BICENTENNIAL EDITION

Lincoln and the Speeds

BICENTENNIAL EDITION

Lincoln and the Speeds

BRYAN S. BUSH

Acclaim Press
MORLEY, MISSOURI

Acclaim Press

ACCLAIM PRESS, INC.
Your Next Great Book
P.O. Box 238
Morley, MO 63767
(573) 472-9800
www.acclaimpress.com

Designer: Ron Eifert
Cover Design: Emily K. Sikes

Publishing Rights: Acclaim Press

Library of Congress Catalog No. 2007943952
ISBN-13: 978-0-9798802-6-1
ISBN-10: 0979880262

Printed in the United States of America
First Printing:
10 9 8 7 6 5 4 3 2 1

Additional copies may be purchased from
Acclaim Press.

This publication was produced using available information. The Publisher regrets it cannot assume responsibility for errors or omissions.

Special Thanks To:

Farmington Historical Home, Louisville, Kentucky
Louisville Free Public Library, Louisville, Kentucky
Filson Club Historical Society
Doug Sikes,
Steve Magruder
My parents: Gene Bush, Jo Ann Bush, Carol Bush

Contents

Abraham Lincoln's Kentucky Connection

On April 15, 1837, a tall, angular young man with lean, wrinkled cheeks and sad grey eyes walked into the general store in Springfield, Illinois, and placed a pair of saddle bags on the counter. He asked the young owner of the store the price of a mattress, blankets, sheets, coverlid, and a pillow for a single bed. The store owner calculated the items at seventeen dollars. The young man replied: "It is perhaps cheap enough, but small as it is, I am unable to pay it. If you will credit me until Christmas, I will pay you then, if I do well; but if I do not, I may never be able to pay you."

The store owner looked up into the face of his customer and said: "You seem to be so much pained at contracting so small a debt, I think I can suggest a plan by which you can avoid the debt and at the same time attain your end. I have a large room with a double bed which you are welcome to share with me."

The customer asked "Where is your room?"

"Upstairs," the owner replied, pointing to a pair of winding stairs which led from the store to the room.

The young man picked up his saddle bags, went upstairs, set them down on the floor, returned below and explained, "Well, Speed, I'm moved!"

The date was April 15, 1837, and the customer was Abraham Lincoln, the generous owner of the store was Joshua Speed, and the friendship that developed between them lasted until Lincoln's death in 1865.

Joshua Speed became Abraham Lincoln's closest friend. The friendship spread to his brother James Speed, who later became Lincoln's attorney general in 1864. Joshua and James also became Lincoln's personal informants on military and civilian activities during the Civil War. With Lincoln's help, Joshua and James Speed helped to save Kentucky for Unionists early in 1861.

The purpose of this book is to present a dual biography of Joshua and James Speed and reveal how closely the friendship between Joshua Speed and Abraham Lincoln continued to affect not only Joshua Speed's life, but also the life of his brother James Speed. Both Joshua and James were dedicated to the Union, even though they followed different paths. James was a Unionist, emancipationist, abolitionist, and Radical Republican. He entered politics, becoming a state representative and later attorney general under Abraham Lincoln and later Andrew Johnson.

Joshua lived his life as a businessman. He differed from his brother and Lincoln on the subject of emancipation, but felt that the issue should not hinder his support of the Union. In April of 1861 after the attack on Fort Sumter, the citizens of Kentucky debated the issue of whether to join the Union or Confederacy. Because of Joshua and James Speed's loyalty to the Union, Lincoln depended on the brothers to help secure Kentucky for the Union. With their help, Lincoln managed to transport thousands of weapons into Kentucky for distribution among the loyal Union Home Guard.

During the war Lincoln needed trustworthy friends to help him deal with the delicate situation in Kentucky. James and Joshua Speed kept him informed on both the political and the civilian affairs. After Lincoln's death, James and Joshua helped to preserve his legacy in their individual ways. James became a Radical Republican and fought to gain equality under the law for blacks, even though most of Kentucky did not want to follow the Radial Republican stance on reconstruction. Joshua helped to maintain Lincoln's legacy by contributing to Lincoln's memorial and speaking and writing about him.

With the 200th anniversary of Lincoln's birth, the story of Joshua and James Speed can give the reader another window into his friendships. The story of Joshua and James Speed can also reveal information about Kentucky politics during the Civil War; the struggle between Union loyalists and Confederate sympathizers, and the struggle for emancipation, abolition, and those who opposed equal rights for blacks in Kentucky.

Many of Kentucky's libraries and public institutions have a good amount of information on the brothers. In 1896, Joshua Fry Speed published a book on his reminiscences of Abraham Lincoln. The book gives a brief look into the friendship between Joshua and his friend Lincoln.

In 1914, James Speed's grandson, also named James Speed, published a book on his grandfather entitled *James Speed: A Personality.* Luckily for the historian, James Speed included a great number of letters written by his grandfather.

In 1936, Helen Springer wrote her master's thesis on James Speed, entitled "The Political Career of James Speed." Springer's thesis was the first scholarly work on James Speed and focused on his political career. Most of her focus was on Speed's career as Attorney General.

In 1943, Robert Kincaid published *Joshua Fry Speed: Lincoln's Most Intimate Friend,* in which the author gave a brief but descriptive life of Joshua Speed. Kincaid separated the book into two parts. The first section of the book covered the life of Joshua Speed and Abraham Lincoln, and the second half included letters written between Joshua Speed and Lincoln.

In 1973, Gary Lee Williams wrote his dissertation entitled "James and Joshua Speed, Lincoln's Kentucky Friends." Williams focused on how Joshua and James Speed played a major role to help keep Kentucky in the Union during the Civil War.

In 2003, Jennifer Cole wrote her master's thesis entitled "Semper Eadem: An Interpretation of the Life and Career of James Speed." Cole tried to work through the inconsistencies in James Speed's political and personal beliefs.

James Speed supported gradual emancipation, but owned slaves. He believed in the Whig Party in the 1840s, but did not follow Whigs into the Know-Nothing Party of the 1850s. At the opening of the Civil War, he joined the Unionists of Kentucky, supporting a Republican administration. His party, the Unconditional Unionist party, pledged their loyalty to Lincoln. Although James Speed was not a Republican, he joined Lincoln's cabinet as Attorney General. Cole stated, that although James Speed was a "southern gentleman," he supported harsh reconstruction and equal political and civil rights for blacks. After resigning his position as Attorney General, he returned to Kentucky to form a Republican Party, which stood for emancipation and Unionism, in a state that did not accept emancipation and radical reconstruction, but supported Andrew Johnson and his National Union Party.

Chapter One

Life on the Plantation

Joshua and James Speed came from a long line of distinguished gentlemen. Their grandfather, Captain James Speed, son of John Speed and Mary Taylor, was born in Mecklenburg County, Virginia, in 1739, and married Mary Spencer of Charlotte County. Captain James Speed served in the American Revolution and received a disabling wound at the Battle of Guilford Court House. For his service in the American Revolution, Congress awarded Captain James Speed with several land grants, totaling around 7,500 acres in the western counties of Virginia, which later became Kentucky.

In 1782 Captain Speed left Charlotte County, in southwestern Virginia and came to Kentucky. With his wife and six children, he crossed the Wilderness Road and settled near Danville, Kentucky. Captain Speed served as a judge. He was also a member of the Kentucky conventions of 1783, 1785, 1787, and worked toward establishing Kentucky as a separate state. In 1792, Kentucky became a state. By that time, Captain Speed owned 45,000 acres of land, most it in central Kentucky and Jefferson County.[1] [See Appendix for information on Farmington and the Speed family]

James Speed, son of John and Lucy Speed, was born on March 11, 1812. Joshua Speed, also the son of John and Lucy Speed, was born on November 14, 1814. Lucy Speed devoted her life to educating her children. Because of the successful hemp plantation, she was able to afford the best education. James Speed attended a small country school, taught by Mr. Smith. He entered Saint Joseph's College at Bardstown, Kentucky, and graduated at seventeen. After graduation he spent time in a clerk's office and moved to Lexington to prepare for law at Transylvania University. When he arrived at Transylvania University and settled in his living quarters, he began to notice the

1 Gary Lee Williams, "James and Joshua Speed: Lincoln's Kentucky Friends," (Ph.D., Dissertation, Duke University, 1971), 5-6.

ladies. He wrote to his family back home "I am much better pleased in every respect than I anticipated, and especially with the ladies of Lexington. Tell my sisters of this and tell them that all they hear there of their stiffness is altogether a bugger."[2] After his graduation from Transylvania in 1833, he returned to Louisville and began a two-year law apprenticeship with local attorney Thomas F. Marshall. After his apprenticeship, he established a law practice with Henry Pirtle, who served as circuit court judge in Louisville from 1826 to 1832.

Joshua Speed also attended good private schools and studied for two years under Bishop Reynolds at Saint Joseph's College in Bardstown, Kentucky. While at Saint Joseph's, he fell ill and quit school. His uncle Thomas took care of him. When he recovered, he rode home to Farmington. His father wanted him to return to college, but he refused, stating he was old enough to make a living on his own. He took a clerk's position in the Louisville wholesale store of William H. Pope. Later, Joshua decided to break out on his own and traveled west. In 1835, he went into business and established a mercantile store in Springfield, Illinois, a town of fewer than 1,500 people.

After establishing his merchant store, he had a meeting with a thin, lanky, man, who was also just starting in his career: Abraham Lincoln. The friendship that evolved in Springfield, Illinois, would forever change the life of not only Joshua Speed, but also the lives of James Speed and several other Speed family members.

---

2 James Speed, *James Speed: A Personality* (Louisville: John Morton & Company, 1914), 2-4.

Chapter Two

Lincoln and Joshua Speed in Springfield

In 1835 Joshua Speed purchased a share in the firm of James Bell and Company and became the manager of the merchant store in Springfield, Illinois, that sold dry goods, groceries, hardware, books, medicines, bed-clothes, mattresses, and other items. In the spring of 1836, Speed heard Abraham Lincoln's first speech, when Lincoln ran for re-election at the county seat. At that time there were two parties: Whigs and Democrats. Lincoln was a Whig and the leading man on the ticket. Speed wrote that he never remembered a more effective speaker: "He carried the crowd with him and swayed them as he pleased."[3]

During Lincoln's speech, a man named George Forquer stood up and asked the people to hear him speak. Forquer had a reputation as a sarcastic but effective speaker. He told the crowd that Lincoln would have to be taken down and he was sorry that he had to do the task. He used sarcasm and ridicule. Lincoln stood near him with his arms folded, never interrupting him.

When Forquer finished his speech, Lincoln walked to the stand and said,

> The gentlemen commenced his speech saying that this young man will have to be taken down, and he was sorry that the task devolved upon him. I am not so young in years as I am in the tricks and trades of a politician; but, live long, or die young, I would rather die now, than, like the gentleman, change my politics, and simultaneous with the change receive an office worth $3,000 per year, and then have to erect a lightning rod

3 Joshua Fry Speed, *Reminiscences of Abraham Lincoln and Notes of a Visit to California*, (Louisville: Bradley & Gilbert Company, 1896), 2.

> over my house to protect a guilty conscience from an offended God."[4]

A former Whig, Forquer changed his party and was appointed register of the land office, and over his house was the only lightning rod in the town or county. Lincoln saw the lightning rod for the first time the day before his speech. He did not understand the function of a lightning rod, so he read a book until he knew all about the purpose of a lightning rod.

On April 15, 1837, Lincoln, a tall angular young man with lean, wrinkled cheeks and sad grey eyes, walked into A. Y. Ellis & Company, Joshua Speed's general store in Springfield, Illinois, and laid on the counter a pair of saddle bags. He asked Joshua Speed the price of a mattress, blankets, sheets, coverlid, and a pillow for a single bed. Joshua Speed calculated the items at seventeen dollars.

Lincoln replied, "It is perhaps cheap enough, but small as it is, I am unable to pay it. If you will credit me until Christmas, I will pay you then, if I do well; but if I do not, I may never be able to pay you."

Speed looked up into Lincoln's face and said, "You seem to be so much pained at contracting so small a debt, I think I can suggest a plan by which you can avoid the debt and at the same time attain your end. I have a large room with a double bed which you are welcome to share with me."

Lincoln replied, "Where is your room?"

The owner replied, "Upstairs," pointing to a pair of winding stairs which led from the store to the room. The young man picked up his saddle bags, went upstairs, set them down on the floor, returned below and explained, "Well, Speed, I'm moved!"[5]

After Joshua's store closed and Lincoln and Speed got to know each other. Speed found that he could not have been any more different from Lincoln. Lincoln told Speed that his ancestors had come from England with William Penn and settled in Pennsylvania. His family moved to Virginia and then to Kentucky. Lincoln was born on February 12, 1809, on the banks of the Nolin River. He went from Kentucky to Indiana, where at the age of ten, he lost his "angel

---

4 Ibid., 3.
5 Ibid., 20.

mother." From Indiana, with his father and step-mother, Thomas and Nancy Hanks, he traveled to Illinois.

He left his father and step-mother in Macon County and moved onto Sangamon County and stopped at New Salem, on the Sangamon River, where he became a boatman and made two trips to New Orleans. While a flatboat man, he studied the subject and invented a machine for lessening the weight on flatboats in order for them to go over shoals. He lived in New Salem for about eight years. While at New Salem, he served as a postmaster, storekeeper, soldier in the Black Hawk War, and as a member of the Illinois legislature at Vandalia. Springfield became the new state capitol, and Lincoln decided to move there. In the spring of 1837, he took his license as a lawyer to become a junior law partner of John T. Stuart.[6]

After his first year in Springfield, Lincoln was known for his skills as a lawyer and became one of the best in the state. He rarely failed in winning his cases in court. Speed pointed out that Lincoln was not a social man and did not seek out company, but many times company sought him out. After Lincoln made his home with Joshua Speed, on long winter nights, near the big wood stove in his store, eight or ten men gathered around the stove to hear Lincoln speak. A social club without organization arose in Joshua's store. Lincoln spoke on any and all subjects except politics.[7]

In 1839, Lincoln drew Speed into Whig Party politics. E.D. Baker, James Matheny, Milton Hay, Joshua Speed and Lincoln wrote a form letter which may have been sent out to other Whig newspaper editors. The form letter stated that Stephen Douglas, a Democrat, intended to run against John Todd Stuart for the Congressional seat. Lincoln knew Stuart in the legislature, which had resulted in a law partnership between the two men. Lincoln, Baker, Matheny, Hay, and Speed informed the Whig Party that they should prepare to meet the challenge.[8] Joshua Speed and Lincoln participated in the Whig Party's state central committee.

On a cold January evening in 1840, a political argument arose between Lincoln and Stephen Douglas. Douglas sprang to his feet

---

6 Ibid. 19-20.

7 Ibid.

8 Roy Basler, *Collected Works of Abraham Lincoln, Volume II*, (The Abraham Lincoln Association, www.hti.umich.edu), 151-152.

and said "Gentlemen, this is not the place to talk politics; we will discuss the questions publicly with you." A few days later the Whigs held a meeting and challenged the Democrats to a joint debate. The two parties took up the challenge. The Democrats sent Stephen Douglas, Lamborn, Calhoun, and Jesse B. Thomas. The Whigs sent Logan, Baker, Browning, and Lincoln. The debate took place at the Presbyterian Church and lasted for eight nights, each speaker talking one night. Lincoln stood on his night, and at the conclusion of his speech said this:

> If ever I feel the soul within me elevate and expand to those dimensions not wholly unworthy of its Divine Architect, it is when I contemplate the cause of my country, deserted by all the world beside, and I standing up boldly and alone, hurling defiance at her victorious oppressors. Here, without contemplating consequences, before heaven and in the face of the world, I swear eternal fealty to the just cause, as I deem it, of the land of my life, liberty, and my love. And who, that thinks with me, will not fearlessly adopt the oath I take! Let none falter who thinks he is right, and we may succeed. But if, after all, we shall fail, be it so; we still have the proud consolation of saying to our consciences, and to the departed shade of our country's freedom, that the cause approved of our judgments and adored of our hearts we never faltered in defending.[9]

Lincoln gave his speech without any notes. His speech filled seven columns of the *Sangamon Journal* and was published as a campaign document.

In mid-March 1840, James Speed wrote to his brother that he planned to marry a "Scottish lassie" named Jane Cochran. He asked for his brother to return home to Kentucky for the wedding ceremony. Ten days later, on March 31, 1840, their father John Speed passed away. Since James was the eldest son, he inherited land and slaves, along with a position as an officer and shares in the Louisville

9 Ibid., 24-25.

Turnpike Company. Although the death of their father had just taken place, James Speed and Jane Cochran married on April 23, 1840.[10]

When Joshua received the news of this father's death, he wrote his mother:

> As I lament the death of a Father, I can but feel more sensibly when I reflect how much beyond measure has been your loss greater than mine. Those virtues that we as his children and you as our mother and his wife loved him for will I hope serve now to enshrine his memory in our heart. . . . If it would be any consolation to you in your affliction to have me with you, you have only to let me know and I will be with you and shed with you "tear for tear."[11]

Joshua Speed encouraged Lincoln to form social contacts. He took Lincoln to parties, attended debating clubs and political forums and took rides into the country. As Lincoln grew as a lawyer, Speed prospered as a merchant. Speed shared Lincoln's broad views on internal improvements and was sympathetic with his ambition to become known as the "De Witt Clinton of Illinois."

Joshua Speed may have introduced Lincoln to Mary Todd in Ninian W. and Elizabeth Edwards' home in Springfield. Ninian and Elizabeth Edwards held Sunday get-togethers at their mansion and invited the best and brightest of Springfield society, including Stephen Douglas, John H. Hardin, Edward Baker, James Shields, and O.H. Browning. The Edwards family included the young and attractive Matilda Edwards, daughter of Cyrus Edwards and Mrs. Elizabeth Edwards' younger sister, Mary Todd.[12]

Lincoln met Mary Todd at one of the Edwards' parties. Their relationship became serious in the fall of 1840, and Lincoln proposed around Christmas of 1840. On January 1, 1841, Lincoln broke off the engagement. There are several different versions of why the break-up occurred. According to Ninian Edwards, Lincoln had fallen in love with Miss Matilda Edwards. He did not tell Matilda that he loved

10 Jennifer Cole, "Semper Eadem: An Interpretation of the Life and Career of James Speed," (Master Thesis, University of Louisville, 2003), 9.

11 Robert Kincaid, *Lincoln Most Intimate Friend*, (Harrogate, Tennessee: Lincoln Memorial University, 1943), 15.

12 David Donald, *Lincoln*, (New York: Simon & Schuster: 1995), 84.

her, but when she became aware of Lincoln's affections toward her, the engagement between Lincoln and Mary Todd ended. According to Ninian Edwards, Miss Todd released Lincoln from the proposal, leaving him the option of renewing the marriage proposal at a later date if he wished. According to Ninian Edwards, Lincoln was conflicted over his sense of duty to marry Mary Todd and his love for Matilda Edwards. Ninian Edwards wanted Lincoln to marry Mary Todd and Joshua Speed to marry Matilda Edwards. According to Ninian Edwards, Matilda Edwards refused Joshua Speed, although no explanation was given in William Herndon's interview with Ninian Edwards, as to the reason why she refused Joshua. According to Ninian Edwards, Matilda refused Stephen Douglas on the account of his bad morals, but again no reason is given in the interview as to what Ninian Edwards meant by "bad morals."[13]

But Lincoln historian David Herbert Donald has a slightly different explanation for Lincoln's breakup with Mary Todd. According to Donald, Mary grew up in luxury, in which family slaves attended to every need. Robert Todd, Mary's father, made sure she had the best education and Lincoln admired the intelligent young woman.

Mary Todd worried about becoming an old maid and searched for a husband. She flirted with Stephen Douglas, but Douglas only had eyes for a Senator's position. She found Joshua Speed handsome and charming, but he had eyes for Matilda Edwards. In Mary Todd's mind, Lincoln became the best prospect for marriage. By the fall of 1840, Lincoln and Mary Todd entered into a serious relationship, and became engaged around Christmas. However, once Lincoln made his commitment to Mary, he began to have serious doubts. He worried about his ability to support a wife. Lincoln earned more than $1,000 a year from his legal practice, plus his salary as a state legislature, but his law partnership with John Stuart was about to end. Lincoln's political popularity also came to an end with the collapse of the Whig improvement system and the bankruptcy of the state. Lincoln would not run for reelection when his term expired. He still owed money from his days in New Salem. He knew he could not afford Mary Todd's life of wealth and luxury.

After his father's death, Joshua Speed decided to move back to Kentucky, so Lincoln did not even have a place to live. With the

---

13 Edward Wilson & Rodney O. Davis, ed., *Herndon's Informants, Letters, Interviews, and Statements about Abraham Lincoln*, (Urbana & Chicago: University of Illinois Press), 133.

mounting anxiety, Lincoln broke down and canceled the engagement.[14] Speed burned Lincoln's letter breaking off the engagement and demanded that he face Mary in person.

Lincoln took Speed's advice and went to the Edwards' mansion to see Mary. He told her he did not love her, and she burst into tears. Mary thought that Lincoln loved Matilda Edwards and wrote Lincoln a letter releasing him from the engagement, but she did not change her mind, about wanting to keep the option open if he wanted to propose again.[15] Lincoln fell into a deep depression over the break-up with Mary.

Speed became concerned with his friend's depression. He said that he had to remove razors from Lincoln's room and took all the knives and other dangerous implements away.[16] He told Lincoln he would die unless he came to his senses. Lincoln told Speed, "I am not afraid, and would be more than willing. But I have an irrepressible desire to live till I can be assured that the world is a little better for my having lived in it."[17] Lincoln wrote to his law partner Stuart that if all humans shared his misery, nobody on Earth would be smiling.[18]

Although Speed would have liked to stay with his friend Lincoln to help him in his deep depression, Joshua had to deal with his own loss. With the recent death of his father, Joshua sold his interest in the store, packed his bags and planned to move back to Kentucky. With heavy hearts, Lincoln and Joshua Speed bid each other goodbye.

---

14 David Herbert Donald, *Lincoln*, (New York: Simon & Schuster, 1995), 86-87.

15 David Donald, 87.

16 Ibid.

17 Roy Basler, *Collected Works of Abraham Lincoln*, 39.

18 Robert Kincaid, *Lincoln's Most Intimate Friend*, 15.

Chapter Three

Lincoln Visits Farmington

As soon as Joshua Speed returned to Kentucky, Lincoln wrote to him. Lincoln wrote about the murder trial of Archibald Fisher, which produced "the highest state of excitement here for a week past that our community has ever witnessed."[19] Speed invited Lincoln to visit him in Louisville, and Lincoln promised to come. In August of 1841, he arrived.

According to legend, Lincoln occupied the big front room on the left of the wide hall. He was assigned a servant for his personal needs from among the slaves. While he stayed at Farmington, Lincoln and Joshua walked the property that surrounded the massive plantation. Joshua rode with Lincoln into the country and he had pleasant chats with Mrs. Lucy Speed. He played children's games with Mary, Joshua's older half sister, and once in a playful mood shut her up in a room to prevent her, as he said, "from committing assault and battery upon me."[20] Lincoln adored Eliza Davis, a niece visiting in the Speed home. He occasionally rode into Louisville where he spent many hours with James, who continued his law practice there. Lincoln read many of James's books and spoke with him "about slavery and the questions of the day."[21] Unfortunately, on one of his visits to Louisville, Lincoln visited a dentist who tried to extract a tooth and failed. Luckily, Mrs. Speed served Lincoln dishes of peaches and cream.[22]

While he was at Farmington, Lincoln tried to forget his unpleasant affair with Mary Todd, but his friend Joshua had fallen in love

19 Roy Basler, *Collected Works of Abraham Lincoln*, (The Abraham Lincoln Association, 1953, www.hti.umich.edu), 255-258.

20 Abraham Lincoln to Mary Speed, September 27, 1841, The Abraham Lincoln Papers, Library of Congress, Washington, D.C.

21 James Speed, *James Speed: A Personality*, (Louisville: John P. Morton & Company, 1914), 50.

22 Abraham Lincoln to Mary Speed, September 27, 1841, The Abraham Lincoln Papers, Library of Congress, Washington, D.C.

with Fanny Henning, who visited her uncle John Williamson, on a farm nearby Farmington. Lincoln rode with friend Joshua on some his visits to see Fanny, but Williamson got in the way for Joshua to do any real courting. One night, Lincoln helped Joshua by monopolizing Williamson's attention in discussion of politics, so Joshua could sneak away with Fanny.[23]

One morning during Lincoln's visit, Mrs. Lucy Speed noticed that Lincoln was moody, and when she knew they were alone, she handed him an Oxford Bible and advised him to read it. She stated that he should adopt the bible's precepts and pray for the book's promises. She made a deep impression on Lincoln, and he never forgot the gesture.[24]

As the summer came to a close, Lincoln and Joshua prepared for their journey back to Springfield, Illinois. They boarded the steamboat Lebanon for St. Louis. On board the steamboat, Lincoln noticed a fine example for "contemplating the effect of condition upon human happiness."[25] He came across a slave owner and his slaves. Lincoln wrote that a gentleman purchased 12 blacks in different parts of Kentucky and planned to take them to a farm in the South. Lincoln noticed the slaves chained six and six together. A small iron handcuff was around the left wrist of each, and the chain fastened to the main chain by a shorter one at a convenient distance from the others, so that the slaves were strung together "like so many fish upon a trout line."[26] Lincoln wrote that in this condition the slaves were separated forever "from the scenes of their childhood, their friends, their fathers and mothers, and brothers and sisters, and many of them from their wives and children, and going into perpetual slavery where the lash of the master is proverbially more ruthless and unrelenting than any other where."[27]

When Lincoln arrived in Springfield, he set out on his circuit to Bloomington and Charleston, Illinois. Joshua stayed with his friend in Springfield until he finished his business affairs and returned to Kentucky on January 1, 1842 to marry Fanny. Joshua Speed had

23 Robert Kincaid, *Joshua Speed: Lincoln's Most Intimate Friend*, (Harrogate: Lincoln Memorial University, 1943), 16.

24 Douglas L. Wilson & Rodney O. Davis, ed., *Herndon's Informants, Letters, Interviews, and Statements about Abraham Lincoln* (Urbana and Chicago: University of Illinois), 158, 342.

25 Abraham Lincoln to Mary Speed, September 27, 1841, The Abraham Lincoln Papers, Library of Congress, Washington, D.C.

26 Ibid.

27 Ibid.

second thoughts about the marriage, and Lincoln counseled him on what to do. Lincoln noticed that Joshua had a "nervous temperament" and his exposure to bad weather on his journey back home proved to be severe on his nerves. Lincoln stated that the absence of all business and the conversation of friends diverted him and gave the mind the occasional rest from the intensity of thought, which sometimes wears an idea "thread-bare and turns it to the bitterness of death."[28] He also pointed out that the rapid and near approach of marriage focused all his thoughts and feelings on the subject. Lincoln told his friend to go through with the marriage "triumphantly, without another "twinge of the soul."[29] He knew that Joshua would tell him that his break-up with Mary Todd applied to the situation, but Lincoln stated that the particular causes did apply in all cases, but the general one, nervous debility, was the key and conductor of all the particular ones and without it they would be utterly harmless, though "it does pertain to you, does not pertain to one in a thousand."[30] Lincoln knew that the problem with Joshua was that he thought he did not love Fanny. Lincoln wrote Joshua as follows:

> What nonsense! How came you to court her? Was it because you thought she desired it; and that you had given her reason to expect it? If it was for that, why did not the same reason make you court Ann Todd [young sister of Mary Todd] and at least twenty others of whom you can think & to whom it would apply greater force than to her? Did you court her for her wealth? Why, you knew she had none. But you say you reasoned yourself into it. What do you mean by that? Was it not, that you found yourself unable to reason yourself out of it? Did you not think, and partly form the purpose, of courting her the first time you ever saw or heard of her? What had reason to do with it, at that early stage? There was nothing at that time for reason to work upon. Whether she was moral, aimiable, sensible, or even good character, you

28 Basler, *Collected Works of Abraham Lincoln*, Lincoln to Joshua Speed, Jan. 3 [?], 1842, 265-266.

29 Ibid.

30 Ibid.

> did not, nor could not then know; except perhaps you might infer the last from the company you found her in. All you then did or could know of her, was her personal appearance and deportment; and these, if they impress at all, impress the heart and not the head.[31]

Lincoln also pointed out that Fanny's "heavenly" black eyes were the reasoning behind the marriage. He pointed out that when he had visited Louisville, Joshua dragged him on a trip all the way to Lexington just to see Fanny Henning.[32]

On February 3, 1842, Lincoln received word from Joshua that Fanny was ill and she was fighting for her health and life. Lincoln tried to console his friend, stating "the death scenes of those we love, are surely painful enough, but these we are prepared to, and expect to see. They happen to all and all know they must happen."[33] He wrote to Joshua that if Fanny Henning died, he wanted to let him know that her death was a great consolation since she was so well prepared to meet death. He hoped that she returned to good health. Lincoln said he should rejoice and not sorrow over Fanny's sickness since his reaction to her illness proved he loved her. Lincoln told Joshua that he alleviated his hypochondria and felt better.[34]

On February 15, 1842, Joshua Speed married Fanny Henning. Lincoln received the news and wrote to his friend that he was "fully convinced that you love her as ardently as you are capable of loving. Your ever being happy in her presence, and your intense anxiety about her health, if there were nothing else, would place this beyond all dispute in my mind."[35]

Again, Lincoln wrote to Joshua on February 25, 1842, that he had opened Joshua's letter "with intense anxiety and trepidation; so much so that although it turned out better than I expected, I have hardly yet at a distance of ten hours become calm." After a discussion of Joshua's foolish forebodings, Lincoln recalled Joshua's previously expressed fear:

---

31 Ibid.

32 Ibid.

33 Basler, *Collected Works of Abraham Lincoln*, Abraham Lincoln to Joshua Speed, Feb. 3, 1842, 267-268.

34 Ibid.

35 Basler, *Collected Works of Abraham Lincoln*, Abraham Lincoln to Joshua Speed, Springfield, Illinois, Feb. 13, 1842, 270.

> "that Elysium if which you have dreamed so much, is never to be realized. Well, if it shall not, I dare swear, it will not be the fault of her who is now your wife. . . . Far short of your dreams as you may be, no woman could do more to realize them, than that same black eyed Fanny. If you could but contemplate her through my imagination, it would appear ridiculous to you, that any one should for a moment think of being unhappy with her. My old father used to have a saying that 'If you make a bad bargain, hug it the tighter;' and it occurs to me, that if the bargain you have just closed can possibly be called a bad one, it is certainly the most pleasant one for applying that maxim to, which my fancy can, by any effort, picture."[36]

On February 25, 1842, Lincoln received word that Joshua planned to stay in Kentucky and would not return to Illinois. Lincoln did not take the news well. He hoped that Joshua and Fanny would move back to Springfield and make their home. He wrote: "I shall be very lonesome without you. How miserable things seem to be arranged in this world. If we have no friends, we have no pleasure; and if we have them, we are sure to lose them, and be doubly pained by the loss."[37]

Joshua and Fanny moved to a country place in the Pond Settlement, 13 miles from Louisville. On March 27, 1842, Lincoln wrote to Joshua that he had no sympathy when Joshua asked advice about how to run a farm. Lincoln stated that he had never owned a farm, nor did he ever expect to have a farm. Lincoln did not study the subject enough to be interested in how to run a farm. He could only tell his friend that he was glad that Joshua was satisfied and pleased with his farm. Lincoln was glad to hear that Joshua was happy. Lincoln reflected back on his "fatal first of January 41," in which he broke his engagement to Mary Todd and how he should be happy, but he remembered that he made Mary Todd very unhappy. He wrote to Joshua that his soul was pained over his break-up with Mary. He

---

36 Ibid., Abraham Lincoln to Joshua Speed, Springfield, Illinois, February 15, 1842, 280.

37 Basler, *Collected Works of Abraham Lincoln*, Abraham Lincoln to Joshua Speed, Springfield, Illinois, February 25, 1842. 280.

stated that his happiness only relied on Mary Todd being happy. He wrote to Joshua that Mary Todd accompanied a large party on the railroad cars to Jacksonville and on her return spoke loud enough so Lincoln could hear her conversation and that she enjoyed her trip. Lincoln stated that he praised God that Mary enjoyed her journey.

Joshua had stated in one of his previous letters that Lincoln was responsible for his happiness. Lincoln wrote to his friend that "God made me one of his instruments of bringing your Fanny and you together, which union, I have no doubt He had foreordained. Whatever he designs, he will do for me yet."[38]

Lincoln told his friend he could not visit him because he was so poor and made so little headway in the world. He advised Joshua of his collecting business. Lincoln sued Branson & Branson in Sangamon County Court. Lincoln won a judgment for $344.79 and costs for Joshua on November 17, 1843. Lincoln informed Joshua that Colonel Robert Allen promised to give a deed of trust to Joshua and made arrangements to pay him, but the value of the money at the Bank of Illinois declined. Robert Allen was the proprietor of stage lines operating out of Springfield and gave his note for $900 at 12 percent to James Bell & Company on January 1, 1842. On July 5, he gave a trust deed of 200 acres in Christian County to Lincoln for use and benefit of Joshua Speed. The Bank of Illinois failed in February 1842, but was expected to resume in June. On June 15, having passed the day set for resumption, the value of its paper declined further. Lincoln wrote to Joshua that he sued William Hall. On September 16, 1842, Lincoln got a judgment by default for $149.65 in James Bell & Company versus William Hall.[39]

On October 5, 1842, Lincoln told Joshua that Shields challenged him to a duel. Although Lincoln filled his days with life on the circuit and in the legislature, he managed to renew his romance with Mary Todd. He needed Joshua's advice as to whether he should marry her. He observed that Joshua had been married for nearly eight months and that Joshua was "happier now than you were the day you married her I well know, for without, you would not be living." He asked Joshua a "closer question: Are you now, in feeling as well as judgment, glad you are married as you are?"[40] Speed must have

38 Ibid., Lincoln to Joshua Speed, Springfield, Illinois, July 4, 1842, 289-290.

39 Ibid.

40 Ibid. Lincoln to Joshua Speed, Springfield, Illinois, October 15, 1842, 303.

given to right advice to Lincoln, because Lincoln married Mary on November 2, 1842.

On January 18, 1843, Lincoln wrote to Joshua that Mary was well and continued her "old sentiments of friendship for you."[41] He said that married life went well with him and his wife and he hoped to see Joshua soon.

Lincoln continued to collect debts owed to Joshua.[42] Two months later, on March 24, 1843, he wrote that William Walters had paid him $703.25 in gold to be given to Joshua. Lincoln wrote further to Joshua that the Whigs met to appoint delegates to the Seventh Congressional District; Lincoln withdrew after seven ballots and Edward Baker was chosen as Sangamon's candidate for the nomination. He told Joshua that Mary was pregnant, but as for the chance that Lincoln might name his newborn after Joshua, he could not exactly say.[43]

In his letter to Joshua on May 18, 1843, Lincoln asked if he possessed houses and lands, oxen and asses, and men servants and maid servants, and having sons and daughters? Lincoln informed Joshua that he and Mary did not have a house, but boarded at the Globe Tavern. His room and board cost only four dollars a week. He wrote that Ann Todd, Mary Lincoln's cousin, had married a man named Campbell, whom Mary said was a "dunce," who had little money or property. Lincoln informed his friend that he would not be able to travel to Kentucky, because he had to attend to business and poverty. He hoped that Joshua and Fanny would come visit him in Springfield. Lincoln told Joshua to tell his mother that if he ever came to visit Louisville again, he would make sure he paid her a visit.[44]

On August 1, 1843, Lincoln's first child, Robert Lincoln was born. Mary named their son after her own distinguished father in Lexington. Joshua and Fanny did not have any children on their Kentucky farm and lived the rest of their lives with no offspring.

Joshua spent his time tending to his thousand-acre farm, growing crops. Eventually Joshua owned 14 slaves to work his farm. Fanny tended to her flower gardens and her roses became famous throughout the countryside. Joshua and Fanny rode together, visited their neighbors, and journeyed to Farmington to visit Lucy Speed. Lincoln

41 Ibid. Lincoln to Joshua Speed, Springfield, Illinois, January 18, 1843, 306.

42 Ibid.

43 Basler, *Collected Works of Abraham Lincoln*, Lincoln to Joshua Speed, Springfield, Illinois, March 24, 1843.

44 Ibid., Lincoln to Joshua Speed, Springfield, Illinois, May 18, 1843, 324.

and Joshua continued to correspond over the next nine years, and their letters contained mostly business matters, which consisted of Joshua's Springfield accounts, notes, and mortgages, which Joshua turned over to Lincoln for collection.[45]

James Speed continued his law practice in Louisville, Kentucky. James became an emancipationist; he disliked the institution of slavery. When the United States contemplated annexing Texas into the Union in 1844, James made up his mind that he was against the annexation as a slave state because Kentucky would become a market for slaves. He wrote that "slavery would not merely be of value as workers or laborers, but would have value as a marketable commodity. Slavery is the curse of the state. I would willingly adopt any feasible plan to be rid of it."[46]

Joshua's and Lincoln's letter writing became less frequent over the next couple of years, but both men had legitimate reasons as to why they could not keep up their correspondence writing. Joshua and James were elected to office in 1847 and 1848, and Lincoln began to raise his family and climb the political ladder.

45 Robert Kincaid, *Joshua Speed: Lincoln's Most Intimate Friend*, 20.

46 James Speed, *James Speed: A Personality*, (Louisville: Morton & Company, 1914), 17.

Chapter Four

James and Joshua Elected to Office

Joshua began his experiment in plantation owning and election to office, while Lincoln continued his political career and raising his family. James began his political career and emerged himself as an emancipationist. As legislators, both Joshua and James had to deal with the amendment to change the Non-Importation Act of 1833, which related specifically with the issue of slavery in Kentucky and Kentucky's new constitution. Although James and his emancipationist supporters tried to support the continuation of the Act and tried to change Kentucky's constitution to support antislavery views, the pro-slavery forces triumphed and defeated James Speed.

On October 22, 1846, Lincoln wrote to Joshua about an explanation of a lawsuit for the collection of an account in which Joshua was involved and that he would like to see him again. He worried about their friendship. He did not receive as many letters from his old friend and wrote that the "true philosophical cause, though it must be confessed, by both of us, that this is rather a cold reason for allowing a friendship, such as ours, to die by degrees. I propose now that, upon receipt of this, you shall be considered in my debt, and under obligations to pay soon, and that neither shall remain long in arrears hereafter. Are you agreed?"[47] He confessed to Joshua that his being elected to Congress did not please him as much as he had expected.

On March 10, he wrote that he had another boy, Edward Baker Lincoln. He wrote that his son Robert Lincoln was "short and low" and always would be and talked plainly. "He is quite smart enough. I sometimes fear he is one of the little rare-ripe sort, that are smarter at about five than ever after." He wrote that Robert Lincoln got into mischief. While he was writing the letter to Joshua, a messenger told Lincoln that Robert was lost, but by the time Abraham Lincoln

47 Roy Basler, *Collected Works of Abraham Lincoln*, Lincoln to Joshua Speed, Oct. 22, 1846, (The Abraham Lincoln Association, 1953, www.hti.umich.edu), 391.

reached the house, Mary had found him, and had him "whipped----and, by now, very likely he is run away again."[48]

In the fall of 1847, Speed met Lincoln and his family in St. Louis, as they were journeying to Kentucky while en route to Washington. Lincoln stopped to see the Todd family in Lexington, but did not stay at Farmington.[49]

In 1847, James Speed was elected to the Kentucky State House of Representatives. He wrote home in 1848 that he was tired of Frankfort and the life he led, but he did not regret having come to Frankfort. He had no time on his hands and had a lot less leisure than when he was at home.[50]

In 1848, Joshua was elected as a Whig to the Kentucky legislature from Jefferson County. Just like his brother, Joshua complained about the trite and boring nature of legislative affairs.[51] At the time, John J. Crittenden was the Governor of Kentucky, General Zachary Taylor was President of the United States, and Lincoln was a member of Congress. John Crittenden was best known as an influential Whig Kentucky Senator, who many thought of as Senator Henry Clay's successor.

Lincoln wrote that Edward Baker was in Washington and wanted to apply for a foreign mission, and that he wished Joshua to try and get Governor Crittenden's recommendation for Baker. Joshua was requested not to apply for a recommendation but to see Governor Crittenden, and in his own way, ascertain what could be done. Joshua informed Lincoln that he had sought a private interview with Governor Crittenden and urged that in view of the great importance of securing the growing State of Illinois to the Whig party, Joshua thought it would be well for General Taylor to confer upon some leading men of the party in the State a foreign mission, adding that on general principles a man who was a Whig in Illinois was a better Whig than one in Kentucky. In Illinois a man had to fight against a majority, whereas in Kentucky he fought with a majority. Governor Crittenden denied that there could be in the world a better Whig than a

48 Ibid.

49 Robert Kincaid, *Joshua Fry Speed: Lincoln's Most Intimate Friend*, (Harrogate, Tennessee: Lincoln Memorial University, 1943), 20.

50 James Speed, *James Speed: A Personality*, (Louisville: John P. Morton & Company, Inc., 1914), 21.

51 Gary Lee Williams, "James and Joshua Speed, Lincoln's Kentucky Friends," Ph.D., Dissertation, Duke University, 1971), 52.

Kentucky Whig, but said he would not dispute on that point. Joshua saw that the great Northwest was to be a power in the land and that Illinois would be the first state among them, and that as a tactician, if the Whigs could gain strength there by giving a foreign mission to some of his friends, he thought that it would be well to do so. Joshua ventured to speak of Baker in very flattering terms. Mr. Crittenden replied that he knew Baker and was not favorably impressed from his limited acquaintance. Crittenden said that Lincoln was a rising man, if he were an applicant he would support him.

By 1848, James Speed hoped to encourage the emancipation clause into the new constitution. On December 30, 1848, the *Louisville Examiner* published an Address on Slave Emancipation. Influential men from both parties signed the address, including James Speed. The address stated that slavery slowed the wealth and population of the state, colonization of slaves was desirable, emancipation sought to preserve the Union, and that emancipation would be beneficial to the state and slave owners because slavery would continue for another 50 years.[52]

Early in February 1848, the House of Representatives introduced a bill which sought to modify the Non-Importation Act of 1833. The Non-Importation Act stated that no slaves could be brought into Kentucky. The Act sought to stop the domestic slave trade into Kentucky and control the slave population and pave the way for emancipation. Pro-slavery men tried to repeal or modify the law, so that citizens living in the state could import slaves for their own use provided they took an oath that they would not import them to sell.[53] The modified act stated that the owners of slaves would have to bear the losses personally if any slave they possessed should be convicted of a felony. James Speed defended the constitutionality of the amendment and added an addition to the modified act that slave owners would have to pay for any damages done by imported slaves. The House of Representatives voted against adopting the amendment and voted to modify the Non-Importation Act of 1833 so that people could import slaves for their personal use but not for the purpose of merchandise. James Speed voted against the modification of the

52 Helen Springer, "The Political Career of James Speed," (M.A. Thesis, University of Chicago, 1936), 14.

53 Jennifer Cole, "Semper Eadem: An Interpretation of the Life and Career of James Speed," (M.A. Thesis, University of Louisville, 2003), 13.

original act of 1833. The pro-slavery men were defeated when the Senate voted down the House bill.[54]

On February 13, 1849, Joshua Speed wrote to Lincoln from the Kentucky House of Representatives that he had met with Governor Crittenden and wanted his opinion upon the talent, capacity and standing of Douglas Breeze and others. Having done this by way of directing his attention to Illinois men, Joshua elicited without exciting distrust an opinion from him as to the capacity of John J. Hardin, Edward D. Baker and Lincoln. Joshua Speed stated that Lincoln was in a higher standing with the Governor than Edward Baker. According to Joshua, Baker's moral weight was not as great as it should be. His career was regarded as erratic, and he was not thought to "possess those patient, plodding, business qualifications so necessary to make a first rate Cabinet officer."[55] He did not believe that Crittenden would exert much influence. He had more confidence in President Taylor's judgment of men than in his own. Joshua thought that Crittenden was going to take a place in the Cabinet. Joshua hoped that Baker would succeed.[56] Joshua had intimated to Lincoln in his letter that if Governor Crittenden's recommendation was of such value as he and Baker both supposed it was, why not apply himself?

Lincoln wrote to Joshua, expressing himself as very much obliged to Mr. Crittenden for his favorable opinion of him. He also thanked Joshua for his kindness, but he would not authorize himself to a first class office and a second class office would not compensate him for being "snarled at by others who want it for themselves."[57]

> I believe that, so far as the Whigs in Congress, are concerned, I could have the General Land office almost by common consent; but then [Martin] Sweet [a Whig from Freeport, Illinois], and [James] Don Morrison [a St. Clair County Whig, who had been United States representative in the 28th Congress], and [Orville H.] Browning, and Cyrus Edwards all want it. And what

54 Helen Springer, "The Political Life of James Speed," (M.A. Thesis, University of Chicago, 1936), 7-8.

55 Joshua Speed to Abraham Lincoln, February 13, 1849, The Abraham Lincoln Papers, Library of Congress, Washington, D.C.

56 Ibid.

57 Roy Basler, *Collected Works of Abraham Lincoln*, Lincoln to Joshua Speed, Feb. 20, 1849, 29.

> is worse, I think I could easily take it myself, I fear I shall have trouble to get it for any other man in Illinois. The reason is, that [Edward] McGaughey, an Indiana ex-member of Congress is here after it; and being personally known, he will be hard to beat by anyone who is not.[58]

In 1849, a repeal bill for the Non-Importation Act reached the House of Representatives. James Speed was no longer a member of the House, but wrote a letter in the *Louisville Courier* stating his concerns about the health of Kentucky. He believed that repealing the Non-Importation Act would allow slave labor to replace free labor in the city of Louisville. The bill passed the Kentucky legislature that altered the Non-Importation Act of 1833 to the point where the act became ineffectual. Joshua Speed voted against the modified act.

After James left Frankfort, he returned to Louisville and continued his law practice. During 1849, he became active in the emancipation movement in Kentucky. On February 1, 1849, a meeting of the emancipationists met in Louisville and on February 14, James Speed read an address to a large audience. Nine days later, emancipationists met in Louisville and appointed a Correspondence and Executive Committee and soon afterward the members appointed James Speed part of the committee. The Committee's purpose was to publish pamphlets and essays related to emancipation. The Committee published at least two pamphlets: *Slave Emancipation in Kentucky* and *An Address to the People of Kentucky on the Subject of Emancipation.*

Slavery Emancipation in Kentucky distanced themselves from the abolitionists in the North. James Speed and the other committee members knew that Kentuckians did not wanted immediate abolition and feared the abolitionists. The pamphlet stated that gradual emancipation increased the wealth and population of Kentucky. The committee stated that population, wealth, manufacturing and industry increased into Ohio and Indiana, because they did not have the institution of slavery. The committee stated that emancipation would be good for free labor.[59] The committee pointed out that the rest of

58 Ibid.

59 Jennifer Cole, "Semper Eadem: An Interpretation of the Life and Career of James Speed," 19.

the civilized world supported emancipation. The committee's final argument rested on the statement that emancipation would preserve the Union.

James Speed supported Kentucky's attachment with the Union.[60] The best solution to rid the state of slavery was through gradual emancipation, since gradual emancipation did not interfere with the right of property or slave and master relations.[61] The committee's plan called for all female slaves born after a certain date to be released when they turned 21, and their children would be born free. The plan would take 50 years allowing for free white labor to replace slave labor.[62]

The pro-slavery forces also met to counteract the anti-slavery forces. In early February a resolution before the Kentucky House of Representatives stated the people of Kentucky were opposed to abolition or emancipation of slavery in any form or shape whatsoever, except as provided by law and the Constitution. The resolution passed unanimously. On February 7, the annual bill to amend the Non-Importation Act of 1833 came before the House of Representatives and stated that slaves should be brought into the state for personal use only. The bill also stated that after five years an imported slave could legally be sold as merchandise. The bill passed the House, although Joshua Speed gave a dissenting vote. The bill went to Senate for ratification and passed by only four votes. The Non-Importation Act came to an abrupt end. The end of the Non-Importation Act meant that slavery and slave trading could continue in Kentucky without any barriers.[63]

On April 28, 1849, an Emancipation Committee assembled in Frankfort, with 150 delegates present from 24 counties. The committee adopted a resolution which stated that they believed slavery was injurious to the prosperity of the state and inconsistent with the fundamental principles of free government; any plan toward emancipation should be supported, including colonization; the importation of slavery should be prohibited, and the citizens of Kentucky should enforce a system of gradual emancipation of slaves. The Convention

---

60 Ibid., 20.

61 Ibid.

62 Ibid., 20-21.

63 Gary Lee Williams, "James and Joshua Speed: Lincoln's Kentucky Friends," 53.

delegates wanted the Non-Importation Act of 1833 to be included in the new Constitution.[64]

The Constitutional Committee chose James Speed as a candidate on the Emancipation Party ticket. On June 14, the Committee selected three men to represent the city of Louisville in the Constitutional Convention. They chose Chapman Coleman, David Beatty, and James Speed. Unfortunately the voters defeated the emancipationist delegates for the Constitutional Convention. Pro-slavery men made sure that the new Kentucky Constitution established and safeguarded the institution of slavery. The proslavery men added a significant clause to the constitution which added that "No slave shall be emancipated but upon the condition that such emancipated slave be sent out of the state."[65] The Kentucky Bill of Rights also added that "the right of property is before and higher than any constitutional sanction; and the right of the owner of a slave and its increase is the same and is as inviolable as the right of the owner to any property whatever."[66] The emancipation movement in Kentucky came to an end; there was no chance in the foreseeable future to end slavery in Kentucky.

After the emancipationists lost in their effort to keep the Non-Importation Act of 1833 and failed to keep slavery out of the new State Constitution, James Speed left politics and returned to his law practice. In 1850, James took on a new law partner when Henry Pirtle took a position to become Chancellor of the Louisville Chancery Court. James served as Louisville Board of Alderman from 1851 to 1854 and served as the Board's president for two years.[67]

Joshua also gave up politics, but not for the same reasons as his brother. Joshua hated his term in Frankfort. Joshua Speed also gave up farming and moved from the Pond Settlement into Louisville to go into real estate business with his brother-in-law James Henning.

Although Joshua Speed gave up political office, his brother could not do the same. Politics was in James Speed's blood, and he did not take long before he sought another political position in the state of Kentucky. Joshua continued his friendship with Lincoln, but they became divided over the issue of slavery, as did the nation.

---

64 Helen Springer, "The Political Career of James Speed," 16.

65 Ibid, 22.

66 Lowell Harrison & James Klotter, *A New History of Kentucky* (Lexington: University of Kentucky Press, 1997), 117.

67 Gary Lee Williams, "James and Joshua Speed: Lincoln's Kentucky Friends," 61.

Chapter Five

Slavery Becomes an Issue

By 1850, James Speed and his fellow emancipationists had failed in their efforts to make gradual emancipation a part of the new Kentucky constitution and the pro-slavery forces managed to further entrench slavery in Kentucky. During the 1850s, James Speed watched as his beloved Whig party collapsed which gave rise to the American Party or the Know-Nothing Party. Joshua Speed continued his friendship with Lincoln, but they differed in their opinion on the issue of slavery. Joshua and James realized that Kentucky was not the only state to deal with the issue of slavery; the rest of the nation also dealt with the issue.

After the Mexican War, sectional antagonisms grew out of the controversies over slavery and the extension of slavery into the new territories acquired from Mexico. Kentucky Senator Henry Clay offered a set of eight resolutions in an attempt to resolve the basic disputes between North and South. For the North, Clay offered the admission of California to the Union as a free state and the prohibition of the slave trade in the District of Columbia. For the South, he proposed that Congress would not interfere with slavery in the District of Columbia or with interstate slave trading. He also proposed a stronger fugitive slave law act.

The new fugitive slave act stated that northern officials had to return runaway slaves to their owners. Any person found guilty of assisting a fugitive slave was subject to six months imprisonment, a $1,000 fine, and reimbursement to the owner for the market value of the slave. The law denied fugitives a jury trial and protection under a writ of habeas corpus. Clay suggested that New Mexico and Utah have no provisions regarding slavery. He proposed that the U.S. government would pay Texas $10 million to settle the state's debts if the state would relinquish certain lands in the New Mexico territory.[68] In September of 1850, Clay's Compromise of 1850 passed the Senate and House. Lulled into believing the nation's problems were solved, the U.S. citizens and their representatives continued their daily lives, but the Compromise of 1850 only bought a fragile peace.

In 1854, Stephen Douglas proposed the Kansas-Nebraska Act. The acquisition of Oregon and California called into question the status of the Great Plains and Kansas-Nebraska Act. The Kansas-Nebraska Act divided the two territories, along the 40th parallel line, along the unorganized land of the Louisiana Purchase. The inhabitants of the territory could vote on whether they wanted slavery without repealing the Missouri Compromise. Southern Congressmen protested, arguing that unless the 36 degrees latitude, 30 degrees longitude line was nullified, slaveholders would be excluded from settling in a large block of land open to free-soilers who would then vote against slavery. Congress repealed the 36 degrees latitude, 30 degrees longitude. On May 30, 1854, the act passed both houses. The act angered the free soil North and cost Stephen Douglas his popularity in the South. Free soil advocates polarized against pro-slavery factions, leading to the formation of the Republican Party.[69]

With the passage of the Kansas-Nebraska Act, Kansas moved toward civil war. Northern abolitionists encouraged settlers to populate the territory in anticipation of a struggle for statehood between pro-slavery and free soil advocates. With the repeal of the Missouri Compromise, pro-slavery factions attacked Lawrence, Kansas, on May 21, 1856, and two days later, the abolitionist John Brown massacred five pro-slavery men at Pottawatomie Creek. President Franklin Pierce sent out Federal troops to calm the insurrection. The pro-slavery and free soil representatives drafted five constitutions before the United States admitted Kansas to the Union as a free state in 1861. During the Kansas uprising, 50 men died over the slavery issue.[70]

In 1852, James Speed took a break from his law practice and traveled to New York, Massachusetts and Rhode Island. Stress and depression led to the trip. James admired the material progress of

68 Bryan Bush, *The Civil War Battles of the Western Theater*, (Paducah: Turner Publishing, 1998, reprint 2000), 6; Patricia Faust, ed., *Historical Times Illustrated Encyclopedia of the Civil War*,(New York: Harper & Row Publishers, 1986), 294.

69 Bryan Bush, *The Civil War Battles of the Western Theater*, 6.

70 Ibid. 7.

the North. After he returned from his trip, he resumed his career as a lawyer. After the Kansas-Nebraska Act ,the Whig party collapsed in the nation, and James Speed was a man without a party. Some of the Kentucky Whigs turned to the Know-Nothing Party or the American Party. The Know-Nothing Party advocated the preservation of the Union, but the party also fought against Catholics and foreign elements in the workforce and Catholics. In 1854, the Know-Nothings won some city elections in Louisville, Covington, and Lexington. Nearly half of the state's total foreign born lived in Louisville. The state's 35,000 Catholics made up about four percent of the population. In 1855, the Know-Nothing candidate Charles Slaughter Morehead won the governorship for Kentucky.

James Speed did not support the Know-Nothings. He wrote to his brother Philip, that he did not support a secret party. "In such a party I see more danger than in slavery; such a party is equally powerful for ill as for good."[71] He did not like the secret tactics used by the Know-Nothings. He wrote to Philip: "My Whiggery has ever taught me to advocate what I believe to be right, and further, that is was as much my duty to do it openly and without fear as to do it at all. . . . The Know-Nothings seem to me to shirk, to keep in the dark. They have no avowed principle, and no declared candidates. It may be that I would advocate or support what they want, but before I do, I must know them as they know me. . . . My Whiggery makes me anti-Know-Nothing. All the noble traits of character that so marked and distinguished its great leader [Henry Clay] forbid my association with such a party."[72]

During the city's elections in August of 1855, the Know-Nothings tried to prevent the Irish and German immigrants from voting. Riots broke out as Know-Nothings beat and shot German and Irish immigrants. German owned taverns and houses were set ablaze on Shelby Street in Louisville. Louisville Mayor Barbee and George Prentice, editor of the *Louisville Journal* prevented St. Martin's Catholic Church from destruction. Know- Nothings managed to find a cannon and headed for William Ambruster's brewery. They stormed the building and set the building on fire, killing 10 Germans in the building who did not escape. The Know-Nothings set to flame Quinn's Row,

71 James Speed, *James Speed: A Personality*, (Louisville: John P. Morton & Company, 1914), 38.

72 Ibid, 36-38.

an Irish tenement, and again burned some of the tenants alive in the dwellings. As night fell, Louisville skyline glowed red from the fires erupting throughout the city. The Know-Nothings won the election. The rioters managed to kill at least 22 people.

"Bloody Monday" proved that the city of Louisville was neither northern nor southern; the city was both. Unlike most southern cities, Louisville had a large foreign population. Unlike Northern cities, Louisville had a black slave population. The city also traded with the North and South. The Know-Nothings could not dispel the issue of slavery or the sectional tensions that arose across the country, but decided to focus their attention on foreigners and Catholics, and Louisville became the perfect breeding ground for the movement.[73]

James Speed became an eyewitness to the "Bloody Monday" riots. He worked in his office until about 5:00 p.m., but before he left the office, he saw many blood-covered Irishmen carried off to jail. He witnessed a crowd yelling down Jefferson Street guarding an Irishman to jail, covered in blood. Between the front gate of the courthouse yard and Sixth Street, the crowd took after a German who was going up Jefferson Street. The crowd struck him several times before he reached the courthouse gate. After he reached the yard, he was knocked down and beaten. To escape the blows, James Speed reported that the man crawled under the Know-Nothings stand, and from where James stood, he saw a man with a iron pitchfork stab the German man under the stand. They dragged the German from under the stand "more dead than alive" and carried him to jail on their shoulders. James reported that he did not see any "foreigner misbehave or do or say an insolent thing."[74]

In 1856, James Speed decided to take a position as a professor at the University of Louisville law school, a position which lasted until 1858. On November 15, 1859, James sent to Abraham Lincoln a pamphlet from Judge Nicholas of Louisville. James wrote to Lincoln that he felt something must be done in the matter, or the United States government would prove a failure. James supported Lincoln's election as a United States Senator even though he was a Republican. He stated that he was a Democrat, but was not saddened by the news.

---

73 George Yater, *Two Hundred Years at the Falls of the Ohio: A History of Louisville and Jefferson County*, (Heritage Corporation, 1979), 69-70.

74 James Speed, *James Speed: A Personality*, 38-41.

James felt that the U.S. citizen's rights and institutions were not in jeopardy in Lincoln's hands.[75]

As for Joshua Speed, he moved from his farm into Louisville and entered the real estate business with his brother-in-law James Henning; the business was successful. Joshua became the wise and careful financier and planner, while Henning became the experienced surveyor and appraiser of property values. As Louisville and Kentucky prospered during the 1850s, Joshua's business expanded and he rose to a prominent position in Louisville's commercial circles.[76]

On August 24, 1855, Lincoln wrote to Joshua Speed on the subject of slavery, the 1850 Fugitive Slave Law Act, and the Kansas-Nebraska Act of 1854. Lincoln admitted that their positions on slavery could not be any more different. He wrote that he disliked slavery and that Joshua admitted the abstract wrong of the institution of slavery, but Joshua wrote he would rather see the Union dissolved than yield his legal right to the slave, "especially at the bidding of those who are not themselves interested." Lincoln wrote back that he was not aware of anyone who was "bidding you to yield that right, very certainly I am not." Lincoln acknowledged Joshua's rights and his obligations, under the Constitution, in regard to Joshua's slaves. He hated to see "the poor creatures hunted down, and caught, and carried back to their stripes and unrewarded toils, but I bite my lip and keep quiet." He recalled the trip he and Joshua took in 1841 from Louisville to St. Louis and the 10 slaves on board the steamboat, shackled together in irons. He wrote that the sight of the slaves' condition onboard the steamboat was a "continual torment" to him and that he saw something like it every time he touched the Ohio, or any slave-border state. Lincoln stated that the subject of slavery made him miserable. He wrote to his friend that he should appreciate how much the "great body of the Northern people do crucify their feelings, in order to maintain their loyalty to the constitution and the Union." He wrote that he opposed the extension of slavery. Joshua wrote to Lincoln that if he were President, he would send an army and hang the leaders of the Missouri outrages upon the Kansas elections:

---

75 James Speed to Abraham Lincoln, Louisville, Kentucky, November 15, 1859, The Abraham Lincoln Papers, The Library of Congress, Washington, D.C.

76 Robert Kincaid, *Joshua Speed: Lincoln's Most Intimate Friend*, (Harrogate, Tennessee: Lincoln Memorial University, 1943), 21.

> If Kansas fairly votes herself a slave state, she must be admitted, or the Union must be dissolved." Lincoln responded to his friend: "But how if she votes herself a slave state unfairly—that is, by the very means for which you say you would hang men? Must she still be admitted, or the Union be dissolved? That will be the phase of the question when it first becomes a practical one. In your assumption that there may be a fair decision of the slavery question in Kansas, I plainly see you and I would differ about the Nebraska law. I look upon that enactment not as a law, but as violence from the beginning. It was conceived in violence, passed in violence, because the destruction of the Missouri Compromise, under the circumstances, was nothing less than violence. It was passed in violence, because it could not have passed at all but for the votes of many members, in violent disregard of the known will of their constituents. It is maintained in violence because the elections since, clearly demand its repeal, and this demand is openly disregarded. You say men ought to be hung for the way they are executing the law; and I say the way it is being executed is quite as good as any of its antecedents. It being executed in the precise way which was intended from the first; else why does no Nebraska man express astonishment or condemnation?[77]

Lincoln wrote that appointed Kansas territory Governor Andrew Reeder was the only man silly enough to believe that fairness was ever intended in the issue of slavery for the state. He felt that Kansas would form a slave constitution and be admitted to the Union. Lincoln stated that every slave taken into Kansas was free, yet the Kansas legislature passed a law to hang men who ventured to inform a black man of his legal rights. Lincoln supported the restoration of the Missouri Compromise, so long as Kansas remained a territory and he opposed Kansas becoming a slave state. Lincoln stated

77 Basler, *Collected Works of Abraham Lincoln*, Abraham Lincoln to Joshua Speed, Springfield, Illinois, Aug. 24, 1855, 321.

that if Kansas became a slave state, he would not try to dissolve the Union. If he and the men who opposed slavery in Kansas succeeded, there would be "enough of us to take care of the Union." Lincoln stated that "if enough men in the North can support your measure, whatever it may be, you can carry the day." He wrote to Joshua of an experience he had in the Illinois legislature when Stephen Douglas introduced the Nebraska bill in January 1855. In February the Illinois legislature called a special session. Of the 100 members comprising the two branches, about 70 were Democrats. The Democrats held a caucus, in which the Nebraska bill was discussed. Only three or more men were in favor of the bill. The masses, both Democrat and Whig, were against the bill, but as soon as the party necessity of supporting it became apparent, "the democracy began to see the wisdom and justice of it." In a day or two, Douglas's resolutions passed by large majorities approving the bill.

Lincoln wrote to Joshua that if the citizens of Kansas fairly voted to become a free state, as a Christian, Joshua would celebrate the passage of the state as free. He stated that all "decent slave holders talk that way, and I do not doubt their candor. But they never vote that way." Lincoln stated that Joshua told Lincoln that he hoped Kansas should be a free state, but he would not vote for any Congressman who would say the same thing publicly. Lincoln pointed out that no man could be elected from any district in any slave state that spoke for Kansas to become a free state. Lincoln thought that slave traders, although a small "odious and detested class," dictated the course of politics for all southerners and "are as completely your masters, as you are the masters of your own" slaves. Lincoln stated that he was still a Whig, but other politicians referred to him as an abolitionist. He said that he voted for the Wilmot Proviso forty times, and no one tried to say he was not a Whig. He only opposed the extension of slavery. He stated he was not a Know-Nothing. Lincoln noticed the rapid degeneracy of the nation. The nation began with the statement that all men are created equal, but the nation "practically read it "all men are created equal, except negroes." Lincoln stated that when the Know-Nothings get control, it will read "all men are created equal, except negroes, and foreigners, and Catholics. When it comes to this I should prefer emigrating to some country where they make no pretense of loving liberty—to

Russia, for instance, where despotism can be taken pure, and without the base alloy of hypocrisy."[78]

As Lincoln closed his letter to Joshua Speed, he mentioned that Mary Todd Lincoln would visit Louisville for a day or two in October 1855. As for the subject of slavery, Lincoln stated that Mary Todd had more sympathy for Joshua Speed than Lincoln did, since Mary Todd came from a family of slave owners.[79]

On September 22, 1859, Joshua wrote to Lincoln that the national horse race course would open in Louisville on October 10, and that some of the country's best horses would compete for the best purses. He also stated that the prettiest women in Kentucky would be present. Joshua invited Lincoln to come to Louisville for the grand opening of the race course unless he was "too old to enjoy either the speed of the horses or the beauty of the women." He invited Lincoln to his house to stay a few days and rejuvenate himself.[80]

Lincoln would soon prepare for the 1860 election. The Southern states feared Lincoln and his Republican party and stated that if Lincoln became President, the Southern states would secede from the Union. When Lincoln won the election, the Southern states held to their promise and began to secede from the Union. Lincoln faced a country at war, and he needed friends to help him keep as many states in the Union as possible. Lincoln turned to his friend Joshua Speed. Even though Joshua believed slavery to be constitutional, he held steadfast to the Union. His brother James came to Joshua's and Lincoln's call to help preserve the Union. The year 1860 became a crucial year for Lincoln, Joshua, and James Speed.

---

78 Basler, *Collected Works of Abraham Lincoln*, Abraham Lincoln to Joshua Speed, Springfield, Illinois, Aug. 24, 1855, 323.

79 Ibid.

80 Joshua Speed to Abraham Lincoln, Thursday, Sept. 22, 1859, The Abraham Lincoln Papers, Library of Congress, Washington, D.C.

Chapter Six

The Presidential Election of 1860

As the nation drew closer to the 1860 Presidential election, Kentucky had to decide whether to vote for Southern Democrats, Democrats, Constitutional Party, or Republicans. The crisis over the state elections in 1859 became a precursor for the national elections. The sectional crisis over the slavery issue tore the Kentuckians apart. Most Kentuckians hoped for compromise, as did Joshua and James Speed. Joshua rejoiced at Lincoln's victory, but knew that the Southern states would no longer listen to Lincoln. He knew that Lincoln would need men to help him preserve the Union and began to secure loyal men. Lincoln trusted Joshua Speed and wanted him in his administration, but Joshua felt that Lincoln could use his help more efficiently in Kentucky.

During the state elections of 1859, Kentucky Democrats divided on whether a federal slave code was necessary to protect slavery. Personal rivalries within the Democratic Party, joined with the dispute over how far the federal government should protect slavery, threatened to tear the Democratic Party apart. Stephen Douglas of Illinois endorsed popular sovereignty, in which the territories allowed the settlers to make the decision as to whether to allow slavery, but "states' rights Democrats" argued that Congress had the power to protect slave property in the territories. They rejected popular sovereignty because they believed the federal government had a legal and constitutional obligation to protect slave property taken into the territories. In contrast, northern Democrats argued that the federal government had no right to decide whether slavery should be allowed in the territories. Kentucky Democrats no longer supported Douglas, because he embraced popular sovereignty. In Kentucky's governor's race, Beriah Magoffin ran against Linn Boyd. Magoffin favored LeCompton and denied that Congress had the power to interfere with slavery in the territories. Boyd was more radical in the defense of southern rights and ran on traditional Democratic ideals. John C. Breckinridge tried to influence the race by nominating former Whigs as Democratic candidates. Doing so, he believed, would win broad support for the party. The "Opposition" Party, which replaced the Know-Nothings, nominated Joshua Bell. The Opposition Party abandoned their anti-Catholic and immigrant stance, and instead appealed to former Whigs by stressing that they would defend slavery against the northern Republicans. They insisted that only federal protection of slavery could restore sectional harmony and preserve the Union. Kentucky Democrats used the memory of Henry Clay to split the Opposition Party. Since Clay's death, the Kentucky Democrats praised him. For example, Democrats denounced Robert Mallory, Opposition candidate for Congress in the Seventh District, because he had been a Taylor candidate in the 1848 Whig national convention, where he had attacked Clay. Magoffin claimed that he and Clay had been the best of friends. Former Whigs were incensed at the Democrats' praise of Clay, because former Democrat enemies of Clay were now praising him. Both the Opposition and the Democrats wanted the former Whig's vote, because old Whig voters still held power in the state even after the death of the Whig party. Clay also symbolized loyalty to the Union above the party or even to Kentucky and most Kentucky voters were devoted to the Union. Although slavery was the key issue in 1859, neither party placed commitment to southern interests over the Union. Kentucky Democrats won the governorship and both houses of the legislature for the first time.[81]

In November of 1860, the nation and Kentuckians cast their votes. Nationally, Lincoln and the Republicans swept the North and with it a majority in the electoral college. John C. Breckinridge, from Kentucky, received 849,781 votes; Stephen Douglas, of Illinois, 1,376,957 votes; Abraham Lincoln, 1,866,452 votes; and John Bell got 588,879 votes. Over 60 percent of the people voted that they did not want Lincoln for President, but Lincoln won enough votes to secure him to electoral college. Bell carried the states of Virginia, Tennessee, and Kentucky. John C. Breckinridge carried the states of Texas,

81 Christopher Paine, "Kentucky will be the last to give up the Union: Kentucky Politics 1844-1861," PhD. Dissertation, University of Kentucky, 1998, 229-230; Harry Volz III, "Party, State and Nation: Kentucky and the Coming of the Civil War," Ph.D. Dissertation, University of Virginia, 1982, 337-338.

Louisiana, Arkansas, Mississippi, Alabama, Florida, South Carolina, Maryland, Delaware, and North Carolina. He got 72 electoral votes, while Lincoln received 180 electoral votes carrying the entire North, as well as California and Oregon. Just as most of the nation voted against Lincoln, so were most of the southern and border states opposed to Breckinridge, largely because of his disunionism. In Kentucky, the Constitutional Party under Bell carried 60 out of 110 counties, a substantial victory.[82]

John Breckinridge ran well in traditional areas of Democratic strength. Bell's votes came from the old Know-Nothings and Whigs. Most Kentuckians did not see why they should switch partisan allegiances. Most Kentuckians agreed that the South and Kentucky should not secede from the Union merely because Lincoln won and in spite of Lincoln's election, most Kentuckians and Kentucky Democrats believed that the political process was the best protectors of their rights. They would not secede. In Kentucky, Lincoln's election was not seen as a mortal threat. The Constitutional Union Party's platform of Union and liberty were the core values of the old Whig party. The party stressed that preserving the nation was the key to maintaining southern rights. Breckinridge Democrats believed that the Union was only valid so long as the government respected southern rights.[83]

How did Joshua and James Speed vote in the presidential election? Unfortunately there is no documentary evidence as to what party the men cast their votes. James Speed may have voted for the Douglas Party ticket since he stated in a letter to Lincoln in 1859 that he was a Democrat. He definitely would not have voted for the Breckinridge ticket, since Breckinridge stood with the secessionists. Although Joshua Speed was a close personal friend for Lincoln, he may have voted for Bell, which stated that Kentucky stood for the preservation of slavery and the preservation of the Union.

In any event, on November 14, 1860, Joshua sent a congratulatory letter to Lincoln on his winning the election as President of the United States. Joshua wrote, "I am rejoiced at your success–as a political opponent I am not disappointed–The result is what I expected."[84] But

---

82 William C. Davis, *Breckinridge: Statesman, Soldier, Symbol*, (Baton Rouge & London: Louisiana State University Press, 1974), 240-241.

83 Ibid.

84 Joshua Speed to Abraham Lincoln, Wednesday, November 16, 1860, Louisville, Kentucky, The Abraham Lincoln Papers, The Library of Congress, Washington, D.C.

Joshua worried about Lincoln winning the election. He wrote that the nation's continuance and the country's future depended upon how much Lincoln dealt with the "inflammable material by which you are, and will be surrounded. The eyes of the whole nation will be upon you while unfortunately the ears of one half of it will be closed to anything you may say—How to deal with the combustible material lying around you without setting fire to the edifice of which we are all so proud and of which you will be the chief custodian is a difficult task."[85] Joshua relayed to Lincoln that he did not seek an office, but would like to see Lincoln and "impart to you some information as to men and public sentiment here which may be valuable."[86] Lincoln agreed to meet with Joshua in Chicago on November 22, 1860, since he had to meet with his new vice president Hannibal Hamlin and other leaders. Joshua took Lincoln's letter with him. He arrived at the Tremont House in Chicago, where Lincoln was staying, but could not get in until he showed Lincoln's letter. When Joshua entered the room, he found Lincoln fatigued. After he complimented Lincoln on winning the election, Lincoln said: "Speed, have you got a room?" Speed told Lincoln he had a room. Lincoln said: "Name your hour, and I'll come and see you. I will bring my wife." Later in the day, Lincoln arrived at Speed's room. He told Speed that Mary and Fanny would stay in the room, while Speed and Lincoln went into Speed's bedroom. After the door was shut, Lincoln threw himself on the bed and said: "Speed, what are your pecuniary conditions—are you rich, or poor?" Speed replied: "Mr. President, I think I know what you wish. I'll speak candidly to you—my pecuniary conditions are good. I do not think you have any office within your gift that I can afford to take." As the conversation between the two men continued, Lincoln focused on the issues facing the nation and wanted a Kentucky representative in his cabinet. Lincoln wanted to make James Guthrie, former Secretary of Treasury under Franklin Pierce, Secretary of War, but he did not want to write to him, so he asked Joshua to ask Guthrie if he might be interested in the position.[87] After Joshua left Chicago, he met with James Guthrie and asked on the behalf of Lincoln

---

85 Ibid.

86 Ibid.

87 Douglas Wilson & Rodney O. Davis, ed., *Herndon's Informants: Letters, Interviews, Statements about Abraham Lincoln*, (Urbana & Chicago: University of Illinois Press), 475.; Robert Kincaid, *Joshua Fry Speed: Lincoln's Most Intimate Friend*, (Harrogate, Tennessee: Lincoln Memorial University, 1943), 21-22.

if he would be interested in the position of Secretary of War. Guthrie stated that the Union must be maintained but refused the position, stating he was too old.[88]

Although Joshua turned down a position in Lincoln's cabinet, he and his brother James Speed became a valuable asset to his administration. Joshua and James kept Lincoln apprised of all military and political events in Kentucky. Lincoln had complete trust in Joshua and James. He soon put their trust to the test by sending weapons to loyal Union men in Kentucky, breaking Kentucky's neutrality.

88 Ibid.

Chapter Seven

War!

"No citizen of the Commonwealth rendered larger or more important and effective service to the Union cause in Kentucky than did that noble gentleman and patriotic citizen, Joshua Speed."–Adjutant General of Kentucky John W. Finnell[89]

"The labors of him [James Speed] and others of like sentiments saved Kentucky to the Union cause and enabled her loyal majority to organize and control."–Civil War historian E. Merton Coulter[90]

On December 9, 1860, Governor Beriah Magoffin addressed a letter to all the slave states in which he advocated a program to protect the states in possession of their slaves and guarantee the recovery of runaway slaves. According to his plan, the Federal government would divide the national territory between slave and free by the 37th parallel line. On December 18, 1860, Senator John C. Crittenden introduced his Peace Compromise, which divided the public domain along the 36′ 30″. On December 20, 1860, South Carolina became the first state to secede from the Union. On December 25, 1860, delegates from Mississippi met with Governor Magoffin to urge a special session of the legislature to plan for the common defense of the South. Delegates from Alabama met with the governor to remind him that the Union had violated their rights and duties and called for the governor to oppose the Union violations. Governor Magoffin called for a convention of all the slave states, where a united program might be devised and their demands given to Lincoln. If the demands failed, then the southern states could as a united force secede. Governor

89 Helen Springer, "The Political Career of James Speed," (M.A. Thesis, University of Chicago, 1936), 34.

90 Ibid.

Magoffin called for a special session of the Kentucky legislature on January 17, 1861.[91] On January 8, 1861, the Kentucky Bell and Douglas leaders held conventions in Louisville. The convention held that Lincoln's election was not a sufficient reason to dissolve the Union. They called for the adoption of the Crittenden Compromise. Preservation and love for the Union was important to the committee, but not at the point of the bayonet. They declared, "that we deplore the existence of a Union to be held together with the sword, with laws to be enforced by standing armies; it is not such a Union as our fathers intended and not worth preserving." The Bell and Douglas followers merged into one party and a "Union State Central Committee" was formed. Among their members were J.R. Harney, W.F. Bullock, George Prentice, and James Speed.[92]

On January 29, 1861, Kentucky Senator Richard Jacob introduced a resolution in the Kentucky House of Representatives declaring that Kentucky should assume the role of peacemaker and restore peace and harmony throughout the land. He stated that Kentucky stood for mediation and compromise. The Kentucky legislature recessed in February to meet again on March 20, 1861. Members of the John C. Breckinridge Democrats became the Southern Rights Party, or States Rights Party. Their opponents were the Douglas and Bell men, who became the Union Democrats. The Southern Rights Party in Kentucky spread Southern propaganda and wanted a state sovereign convention.

On February 22, 1861, the pro-Union citizens of Louisville decided to celebrate George Washington's birthday with a celebration. The event took on a whole new meaning with the political affairs. The citizens of Louisville decided to raise the national flag with pomp and circumstance over the Jefferson County courthouse. Fifty thousand people attended the event at the courthouse. At 2:30 p.m. the Louisville Battalions formed on Jefferson Street, fronting the courthouse. After a short prayer, James Speed delivered a patriotic speech. In his speech, he told the crowd:

---

91 Merton Coulter, *The Civil War and Readjustment in Kentucky*, (Chapel Hill: University of North Carolina Press, 1921, reprint Glouster, Mass, 1966), 27.

92 E. Merton Coulter, *The Civil War and Readjustment in Kentucky*, (University of North Carolina Press, 1926, reprint 1966), 28.

> In contemplating the causes which may disturb our Union, it occurs as a matter of serious concern, that any ground should have been furnished for characterizing parties by geographical discriminations, Northern and Southern, Atlantic and Western, whence designing men may endeavor to excite a belief that there is a real difference of local interests and views. One of the expedients of party to acquire influence, within particular district, is to misrepresent the opinions and alms of their districts. You cannot shield yourself too much against the jealousies and heart burnings which spring from their misrepresentations. They tend to alien to each other those who ought to be bound together by fraternal affection. . . . To the efficacy and permanency of your Union, a Government for the whole is indispensable. No alliance however strict between the parts can be an adequate substitute.
>
> And now our flag of our country what shall, what can I say equal to what we all feel. It seems surrounded with peril, and is threatened to be rent in twain. Men of America, be not discouraged! A cloud of prejudice and a storm of passion may for a time obscure its luster, but the cloud will vanish, the storm must abate, and as when the tempest is the material world is passed, and we look out and up, we find the heavens all star-studded, so when the political clouds and storms now about us shall pass away, we will find the flag of our country floating proudly on the breeze, bright and enduring as the heavens above.[93]

At the end of James Speed's speech, Colonel J.H. Harvey and George D. Prentice raised the national flag over the courthouse. Colonel William Woodruff and the Marion Rifles fired three volleys from their muskets. When the citizens of Louisville raised the flag, General Simon B. Buckner, commander of Kentucky State Guard, gave no order to salute, as required by the published program and

93 *The Louisville Daily Democrat*, Feb. 22, 1861.

patriotic duty. Buckner and a large portion of his command moved from the Jefferson County courthouse yard. Major William Woodruff of the Marion Rifles, a Louisville militia company, saluted the national colors.[94] Divisions among the Kentucky State Guard and the local pro-Union militias began to divide over which side the state would chose, either Union or Confederate.

On March 20, a Southern Rights Convention met, but failed to influence the state legislature. The Kentucky legislature adjourned on April 4, without calling for a sovereign convention.

On April 12, 1861, the Civil War began with Confederate General P.G.T. Beauregard firing upon Fort Sumter, in the Charleston, South Carolina, harbor. Fort Sumter, commanded by Union General Robert Anderson, surrendered to the Confederates. Kentucky declared its neutrality. Three days later Lincoln called for 75,000 troops and the Secretary of War informed the Governor of Kentucky Beriah Magoffin that four regiments of militia should be raised for the Union. Magoffin wrote back to Secretary of War Simon Cameron that "Kentucky will furnish no troops for the wicked purpose of subduing her sister Southern states."[95] On April 17, the Union State Central Committee promised to defend the state if invaded, but also would not stand by and see other Southern states invaded by the Union. "What the future duty of Kentucky may be, we, of course, cannot with certainty foresee, but if the enterprise announced in the proclamation of the President should at any time hereafter assume the aspect of a war for the overrunning and subjugation of the seceding states through the full assertion therein of the national jurisdiction by a standing military force, we do not hesitate to say that Kentucky should promptly un-sheath her sword in behalf of what will have then become her common cause."[96] On April 19, James Speed and other Unionist members called for a meeting in Louisville. Five thousand men attended the meeting and declared neutrality, but the delegates could not agree on secession in case of coercion.

But neutrality was slowly falling apart. Throughout the state, individuals and groups left to join the Confederacy in Virginia or Tennessee. On April 20, 1861, two companies from Louisville, under

94 Thomas Van Horne, *The Army of the Cumberland*, (New York: Smithmark Publishers, 1996, original printing, 1875), 2-3.

95 Coulter, *The Civil War and Readjustment in Kentucky*, 38.

96 Ibid., 44.

the command of Captains Ben Anderson and Fred Van Osten left for New Orleans and were later joined by Captain Jack Thompson's company and became the Third Kentucky battalion. On April 25, Captain Joe Desha and 100 men from Harrison County, along with three companies from Louisville under Captains John Pope, J.B. Harvey and M. Lapielle, left the state to join the Confederate army. They were joined in Nashville by two companies from southwest Kentucky under Captains Edward Crossland and Brownson. Others joined the Union army in Indiana or Ohio.[97]

In April 1861 Kentucky took out loans to pay for arms. The money was to be used "for arming the State for self defense and protection, to prevent aggression or invasion from either the North or South, and to protect the present status of Kentucky in the Union."[98]

Governor Magoffin refused the Confederate call for troops from Kentucky, but many Kentuckians joined the Confederacy anyway. On May 15, 1861 a Confederate regiment was formed at Harper's Ferry, Virginia, under Colonel Blanton Duncan. General Simon Bolivar Buckner, commander of the Kentucky State Guard, maintained that the Kentucky State Guard was to remain neutral in the conflict and protect Kentucky from both factions, but since many of the State Guard were pro-Southern in sentiment, large numbers of the Guard resigned and joined the Confederacy. The Kentucky legislature ordered the organization of the enrolled militia into companies, to be called Home Guards, for home and local defense.[99]

Lincoln knew the importance of Kentucky and did not want to push the state into the other camp, so he treated Kentucky with a gentle hand. Lincoln made the statement that "I think to lose Kentucky is nearly the same as to lose the whole game. Kentucky gone, we cannot hold Missouri, nor, I think, Maryland." Even though Kentucky's neutrality aided the Confederacy, Lincoln did little to stop the shipments of military supplies heading south by rail and river. In May, Lovell H. Rousseau and Lieutenant William "Bull" Nelson, a commander in the United States Navy who was from Maysville, worked together to strengthen the Union cause in Kentucky.

Lieutenant Nelson gained an interview with Lincoln, and they

97 The Military Department of Kentucky, The Military History of Kentucky, (The American Guide Series, Works Projects Administration, 1939), 153; Coulter, The Civil War and Readjustment in Kentucky, 48.

98 *Military History of Kentucky*, 153.

99 Ibid., 154-155.

discussed the situation in Kentucky. The President worried about the possibility of the well-armed State Guard under Simon Buckner being transferred to the Southern cause, leaving the loyal citizens of Kentucky without a means of enforcing the will of the Union-held legislature. Nelson persuaded Lincoln to send arms to Union sympathizers in Kentucky. Lincoln arranged for 5,000 guns to be secretly shipped from Washington, D.C., to Louisville, with Nelson carrying out the mission. Lincoln charged Salmon Chase with the care of Nelson's work, drawing up his orders and providing the money to buy the weapons. On May 4, Nelson left with the guns by train for Louisville. At Cincinnati, he sent 1,200 guns by steamboat to Jeffersonville, Indiana. Nelson arrived by train in Louisville, leaving the remainder of the guns in Cincinnati. Lincoln directed Nelson to meet with Joshua Speed for the distribution of the weapons.[100]

Nelson arrived at Joshua Speed's home on Second Street, between Liberty and Walnut, but hesitated for a moment, then walked on. Several steps down the street, he turned around and headed back for Joshua Speed's house, only to pass by the house again. Inside the house, Mrs. Fanny Speed and the servants became alarmed at Nelson pacing back and forth in front of their window. After Nelson made sure that he was not being followed, he knocked on Joshua's door. One of the servants informed Nelson that he was in his office, several blocks away, on Jefferson Street between Fourth and Fifth Streets. When Nelson arrived at Joshua's office, he shut the door and asked if they were alone. Joshua assured him that no one else was in the room. Nelson asked if they might move into another room in the office. Joshua agreed. Nelson introduced himself and announced his instructions from Lincoln. He explained his shipments of weapons and hoped Joshua would be able to distribute the guns to Unionists in the state.[101]

Joshua agreed to help distribute the weapons and decided that a Unionist strategy session must take place that evening. Accompanied by his brother James, Joshua Speed left for Frankfort that

---

100 Gary Lee Williams, "James and Joshua Speed: Lincoln's Kentucky Friends," (Ph.D. Dissertation, Duke University, 1971), 86; Thomas Van Horne, *The Army of the Cumberland*, (New York, Smithmark Publishers, 1996, original printing 1875), 11.

101 Williams, "James and Joshua Speed: Lincoln's Kentucky Friends," 87.; Robert Kincaid, *Joshua Fry Speed: Lincoln's Most Intimate Friend*,(Harrogate, Tennessee: Lincoln Memorial University, 1943), 23.

afternoon by train, but traveled separately from his brother and Nelson, so as not to arouse suspicion. None of them spoke to each other on the train. Upon arrival to the Capitol Hotel, in Frankfort, Nelson visited a friend's house, while Joshua sent notice of their arrival and plans to several prominent Unionist leaders.

At 9:00 p.m., Nelson, James, and Joshua met with James Harlan, John J. Crittenden, Charles Wickliffe, Garrett Davis, and Thornton Marshall. The members agreed to the plan for arming Kentucky Unionists. Nelson thought that the guns should be brought into the state immediately, openly if necessary. The others disagreed, pointing out that the shipment of weapons into the state was illegal and might prove embarrassing to the Union cause. Joshua suggested that the operation remain secret until enough of the weapons had been placed in the right hands in order to secure Kentucky's future within the Union. The members agreed and decided that Joshua should make the arrangements for the distribution of the weapons and that all orders for weapons given by selected men in various sections of the state must be countersigned by him. The members agreed that each member should be assigned a district, in which to distribute the weapons. In addition, the members agreed to send James Speed to Indianapolis to obtain ammunition from Governor Oliver P. Morton. Morton met with James and agreed to supply ammunition to Jeffersonville, Indiana.[102]

Nelson moved the shipment of weapons from Jeffersonville to the basement of the Jefferson County courthouse. He also sent a small shipment of weapons to Shelbyville, about 40 miles southeast of Louisville and Hopkinsville, Kentucky. Nelson moved the weapons in Cincinnati to Covington. On May 17, after the weapons arrived in Covington, Nelson transported the weapons by train bound for Cynthiana, Paris, and Lexington. After the train arrived at the various depots, Unionists would distribute the weapons to other parts of the state.

Southern sympathizers at Cynthiana learned of the shipment of "Lincoln guns" arriving at their depot and decided to capture them. As the train approached the depot, the conductor saw the huge crowd and stopped the train and returned to Covington, where the weapons were divided again, some being sent to Maysville, the rest remaining

102 Williams, 88.; Robert Kincaid, 24.

in Covington. Unionists sent the guns in Maysville to various points in central Kentucky by wagon.[103]

Unofficially Joshua and James Speed became Lincoln's informants on the state of affairs in Kentucky. On May 14, 1861, Lincoln wrote to General Robert Anderson, hero of Fort Sumter, native Kentuckian, and soon to be commander of the Military Department of Kentucky, that James Guthrie, John Crittenden, and Joshua Speed distributed the arms from Cincinnati to Unionists' hands. Lincoln thought that Anderson could perform the same duties just as safely and more expeditiously. He also told Anderson that Joshua Speed, Guthrie and Crittenden could provide valuable assistance to him in the distribution of arms and other matters. Lincoln wrote that Joshua Speed was "less known to the world than other gentlemen, [and] is far better known to me than either of them: I have the utmost confidence in his loyalty and integrity, and also in his judgment on any subject which he professes to understand."[104] Lincoln wrote to Anderson that Joshua could provide "valuable assistance in our common cause."[105]

On May 19, 1861, General Robert Anderson wrote to Lincoln that he received his letter introducing Joshua Speed and his instructions about issuing arms to their friends in Kentucky. Joshua Speed advised Anderson not to raise troops in Kentucky. The Committee would be in charge of raising troops and would arm the Home Guard.[106]

On May 24, 1861, Joshua wrote to Joseph Holt, Secretary of War and later Judge Advocate General, that the people of Kentucky were still loyal to the national government, but they distrusted the Lincoln administration and their reasons for prosecuting the war. Joshua stated that "if they can be convinced that this is no war upon individual property and the institution of slavery, we would be almost a unit for the Government. Public opinion is fast settling down in that way—and I think we can keep her as she is—notwithstanding all the efforts of the Governor and the clique at Frankfort. For heaven's

---

103 Williams, 89.; Coulter, 89.

104 Roy Basler, *Collected Works of Abraham Lincoln*, Volume 4, Abraham Lincoln to Robert Anderson, May 14, 1861, Washington, D. C., (The Abraham Lincoln Association, 1953, www.hti.umich.edu), 369.

105 Ibid.

106 Robert Anderson to Abraham Lincoln, May 19, 1861, The Abraham Lincoln Papers, Library of Congress, Washington, D.C.

sake aid us if you can."[107] Joshua wanted Holt to return to Kentucky and give pro-Union speeches. Holt complied with Joshua's request, but his letter opposed neutrality and bitterly castigated the South. He added that neutrality was better than rebellion. He stated that neutrality was untenable and that the United States had every right to pass into or through Kentucky. Holt declared that the Federal troops would resist aggressions in no spirit of malice or destructiveness. He wrote: "If called on to press her soil they will not ruffle a flower of her gardens, nor a blade of grass of her fields in unkindness. No excesses will mark the footsteps of the armies of the Republic; no institution of the States will be invaded or tampered with; no rights of persons or property will be violated."[108] He stated that the South refused to compromise and that the South attempted to drag Kentucky to fight their battles. He also wrote that if Kentucky "should join the Confederacy she would be taxed to death, and soon find herself [a] dangling thread of the raveled Southern fabric; for the Confederacy would inevitably fall apart."[109] Joshua Speed printed Holt's letter as a pamphlet and distributed 30,000 copies across the state.[110]

The 5,000 weapons sent to Captain William Nelson for distribution to loyal Unionists ran out, and he asked Joshua Speed for more weapons. Joshua wrote to Lincoln asking for more weapons. On May 27, 1861, Joshua Speed wrote to Lincoln that the small number of weapons had a "most salutary influence upon the party in Ky.—giving strength and confidence to our friends—and weakening our foes."[111] He informed Lincoln that only reliable men who swore to support the U.S. Constitution would receive the arms, and that if "the good work can go on—without bloodshed or violence we will have Kentucky all right—So far we have beaten them in their own game."[112] He informed Lincoln that Governor Magoffin had borrowed $60,000 from the Bank and dispatched an agent to New Orleans to buy weapons. The Governor dispatched a message to Louisville informing Joshua that he had made a purchase of arms and they would arrive in Louisville. The secessionists boasted of what they intended to do

107 Joshua Speed to Joseph Holt, May 24, 1861, Joseph Holt Papers, Library of Congress, Washington, D.C.

108 Merton, *The Civil War and Readjustment in Kentucky*, 93-94.

109 Ibid. 94.

110 Ibid.

111 Joshua Speed to Abraham Lincoln, May 27, 1861, The Abraham Lincoln Papers, The Library of Congress, Washington, D.C.

112 Ibid.

with the arms. The arms arrived, but the weapons turned out to be old flintlocks altered to percussion, and the weapons did not even have a touch hole in the bore. Joshua wrote that the men "could load them very well but d—n [if not] the one would go off." He stated to Lincoln that the best of the joke was that the guns belonged to some "Yankee and entrusted to George Saunders to sell—who had offered them at $1.25 each and could not find a purchaser—They were sold to our Governor at $8.50 each—the agent I suppose pocketing the difference—The joke was so good a one that the lovers of fun could not keep it." He asked Lincoln for more arms, and if the Union men did not get the arms, "we will in all probability have to run the gauntlet for our lives."[113]

The next day, James Speed, Joshua Speed, Charles Wickliffe, Garrett Davis, J.H. Garrard, James Harlan, Thomas Marshall, James F. Robinson, M.B. Huston, John Goodloe, and J.B. Bruner wrote to Lincoln that their private committee had distributed the arms brought to Kentucky by William Nelson, to true and reliable Union men. The committee assured Lincoln that all of the 5,000 muskets and bayonets had been distributed to the Union men who swore to support the Constitution and the enforcement of the laws and if the occasion should arise, to use them to put down all attempts to take Kentucky by violence or fraud out of the Union. The committee informed Lincoln that the arms greatly added to the sense of security and confidence that they could hold Kentucky in the Union. The possession of the arms in the hands of Union men held to repress the secessionist's violence and hectoring and improved the Union feeling in the northern portion of the state. The committee wrote to Lincoln that thousands of men applied for arms and they had no doubt that 20,000 arms could be entrusted to loyal Unionists, and that these men could hold the state in the Union. The committee promised Lincoln that the government would have true men and faithful agents.[114]

On June 2, 1861, Joshua wrote to Lincoln stating that he had met General Robert Anderson at his headquarters in Cincinnati, where he learned that Union authorities had ordered Anderson to aid the surveyor of the port of Louisville in prohibiting the passage of supplies destined for the Confederacy. The governors of Ohio, Indiana,

---

113 Ibid.

114 Charles Wickliffe, et al to Abraham Lincoln, May 28, 1861, The Abraham Lincoln Papers, Library of Congress, Washington, D.C.

and Illinois protested the illegality of the trade and called for federal intervention. Joshua Speed stated to Lincoln that if General Anderson carried out his orders, the Unionists would be lost in the coming elections. He asked Lincoln to allow the Louisville Home Guard to look into the matter and enforce any control over the port.[115]

Lincoln responded to Joshua's request for more weapons, and on June 5, 1861, he sent another 5,000 weapons. Two days later, Joshua Speed wrote to Lincoln introducing Captain Lovell Rousseau of Louisville, a Kentucky state senator, prominent member of the bar, and commander of the Home Guard. He was also a friend of Joshua Speed. Joshua informed Lincoln that Rousseau was an "intense Union man" and very intelligent gentlemen.[116] Upon Joshua Speed's introduction, Lovell left for Washington to meet with Lincoln. Lovell hoped to impress upon Lincoln the necessity of enlisting troops for the Union army and to request authority to raise one or more regiments in Kentucky. Secretary of the Treasury Salmon P. Chase obtained a Colonel's commission for Rousseau and authorized him to raise two regiments.[117]

Upon Rousseau's return from Washington, he met with General James Speed, with instructions from Lincoln, to call a meeting at Louisville, to determine the location of Rousseau's camp. James Guthrie, Garrett Davis, C.D. Pennabaker, Samuel Gill, James Speed, Joshua Speed, Samuel Lusk, Jeremiah Boyle, Morgan Vance, Thomas Bramlette, E. Graves, A.B. Hobson, J.H. Ward, and James Harlan, along with Colonels Hawkins, Dudley, and Rousseau attended the special meeting. James Speed, Vance, Ward, and Rousseau wanted to establish the camp in Kentucky. The majority feared that if they established a camp in Kentucky, the consequences could cost the congressional election, so they decided to locate the camp in Indiana, on the north bank of the Ohio River, between Jeffersonville and New Albany, and name the camp "Joe Holt."[118]

On June 20, 1861, Kentucky held the special Congressional election. Unionist sentiment dominated the state, so most of the

115 Joshua Speed to Abraham Lincoln, June 2, 1861, Robert Anderson Papers, Library of Congress.

116 Joshua Speed to Abraham Lincoln, June 7, 1861, The Abraham Lincoln Papers, The Library of Congress, Washington, D. C.; Robert Kincaid, *Joshua Speed: Lincoln's Most Intimate Friend*, 24.

117 Thomas Van Horne, *The Army of the Cumberland*, (New York, Smithmark Publishers, 1996, original printing, 1875), 14.

118 Ibid.

Southern Rights men did not place votes in the election. The result of the election was an overwhelming victory for the Unionists. The Southern Rights Party received majorities in only 15 counties and mostly in the western part of the state.[119]

On July 2, 1861, Lieutenant William Nelson established Camp Dick Robinson, between Danville and Lexington, Kentucky. Nelson raised 2,000 men. Governor Beriah Magoffin demanded that Lincoln remove the camp. Lincoln stated that the people of Kentucky wanted the camp and refused to comply with Magoffin's request. The 3rd, 4th, 7th Kentucky regiments, and the 1st Kentucky Cavalry, under the commands of Colonels Thomas Bramlette, Speed S. Fry, T.T. Garrard, and Frank Wolford organized at Camp Dick Robinson.[120]

On July 10, 1861, Lovell Rousseau resigned as commander of the Louisville Home Guard and began to organize Union troops at Camp Joe Holt, across the river from Louisville near Silver Creek, Jeffersonville, Indiana. James Speed accepted the position of brigadier general of the Louisville Home Guard and the mayor of Louisville, John Delph became commander-in-chief of the Louisville Home Guard. On July 21, after the Battle of First Bull Run in Manassas, Virginia, James and Joshua Speed traveled to Lexington to secretly meet with General William Nelson, Garrett Davis, James Harlan, Sr., Jerry Boyle, and Colonel T.T. Garrard. When the brothers returned to Louisville, the city was in a state of excitement. James called out the Home Guard to prevent the outbreak of rebellion in the city.[121]

On August 5, James Speed left Louisville to take a seat in the Kentucky State Senate after Rousseau vacated the position. He beat Jeff Brown by a margin of 4,788 to 605 votes. The state elections in August reflected the state's position on Unionism. Of the 19 senators elected in Kentucky, only one claimed to be a secessionist. In the House of Representatives, the Unionists gained 76 seats while the Southern Rights Party won 24 seats. In the Kentucky Senate, the Unionists won 27 seats, while the Southern Rights Party won 11 seats.[122]

Ten days later, the Unionists and secessionists formed a peace committee. James Speed ran against James Trabue, a secessionist,

---

119 Merton, *The Civil War and Readjustment in Kentucky*, 95.

120 Thomas Van Horne, *The Army of the Cumberland*, (New York: Smithmark Publishers, 1996, original printing, 1875), 18.

121 Williams, "Joshua and James Speed: Lincoln's Kentucky Friends," 96.

122 Merton, *The Civil War and Readjustment in Kentucky*, 97.

for the chairman position. When James Speed suggested that those in favor of himself as chairman go to the right and those in favor of Trabue move to the left, many of the members of the committee moved to the right. The secessionists walked out of the meeting.[123]

On August 15, the Union army extended General Robert Anderson's command to encompass the states of Kentucky and Tennessee, under the title of the "Department of the Cumberland." Open recruitment of Union troops took place at Camp Dick Robinson, and General Robert Anderson took command of the gathering Union forces in Kentucky and set up his headquarters in Louisville.

On August 20, the Union Central Committee endorsed a plan to Lincoln to station troops opposite Paducah, Kentucky. On August 24, James Speed, along with the rest of the Union Central Committee, Mayor John Delph, and the District Chief of Police, asked that Colonel Lovell Rousseau's regiment remain in Indiana. General John Fremont of Missouri ordered Colonel Rousseau to Missouri. General Fremont planned to occupy Columbus, Kentucky, and began to assemble Federal troops in Missouri for the occupation. The next day on August 25, Joshua wrote to Lincoln asking that he countermand General Fremont's order stating that Colonel Rousseau was to leave for St. Louis. Lincoln countermanded Fremont's order.[124]

On September 1, 1861, Joshua Speed wrote to Abraham Lincoln about the affairs in Kentucky. He met General Anderson and discussed Kentucky matters. Anderson and Joshua Speed knew that Tennessee had spies in the Southern counties of Illinois, Indiana and Ohio to see how much opposition against the federal government existed and whether those states were in a condition to render the Union men in Kentucky any assistance, should the South make an advance into Kentucky. Louisville sent commissioners to each of the Governors of Illinois, Indiana and Ohio to advise them about the spies. Governor William Dennison of Ohio promised Kentucky that his troops would be ready to assist the state at any moment.

123 Helen Springer, "The Political Career of James Speed," (M.A. Thesis, University of Chicago, 1936), 45-46.

124 Jennifer Cole, "Semper Eadem: An Interpretation of the Life and Career of James Speed," (M.A. University of Louisville, 2003), 31; J.H. Harney and James Speed to Abraham Lincoln, August 20, 1861, The Abraham Lincoln Papers, The Library of Congress, Washington D.C.; Bland W. Ballard, et. al to Abraham Lincoln, August 24, 1861, The Abraham Lincoln Papers, The Library of Congress; Joshua Speed et. al to Abraham Lincoln, August 25, 1861, The Abraham Lincoln Papers, The Library of Congress.

Governor Oliver Morton of Indiana and Governor Richard Yates of Illinois were to meet with Joshua Speed and General Robert Anderson. Joshua informed Lincoln that Kentucky would give the rebels a good fight, but with traitors and enemies in Kentucky, and a disciplined army from Tennessee advancing, Kentucky needed help. He thought that Anderson would soon have an army of 20,000 men.[125]

He also wrote to Lincoln that he read General John Fremont's proclamation, issued on August 30, 1861, which freed the slaves owned by secessionists in Missouri. Joshua Speed felt that his proclamation would hurt Kentucky. In his opinion the war should be waged upon "high points and no state law be interfered with." He wrote, "Our constitution and laws both prohibit the emancipation of slaves among us—even in small numbers—If a military commander can turn them loose by the thousands by mere proclamation—It will be a most difficult matter to get our people to submit to it."[126] He informed Lincoln that those who live in slave states, whether Union or loyal, feared a slave insurrection. He feared that the slaves would read Fremont's proclamation and it would incite them to insurrection and assert their freedom. He stated that the community, including the owner, whether loyal or not, would suffer from the proclamation. He wrote that the proclamation was "directly against the spirit of the law."[127] In a lighter note, Joshua Speed asked Lincoln if he had received the six Kentucky hams he sent by mail.[128]

The next day, on September 2, 1861, James Speed wrote to President Lincoln informing him that the large majority of Kentuckians and the Kentucky legislature condemned General Fremont's proclamation. He hoped that Lincoln would not authorize it.[129] The next day, Joshua sent another letter to Lincoln stating that Fremont's proclamation distressed him to the point where he could not eat or sleep. He worried that the proclamation would crush out every "vestige of a Union party in the state—I perhaps and a few others will be left alone—for I do not intend that the act of any military chieftain or any

125 Joshua Speed to Abraham Lincoln, September 1, 1861, The Abraham Lincoln Papers, The Library of Congress, Washington, D.C.

126 Ibid.

127 Ibid.

128 Ibid.

129 Green Adams and James Speed to Abraham Lincoln, September 2, 1861, The Abraham Lincoln Papers, The Library of Congress, Washington, D.C.

administration shall drive me from my fidelity to my government."[130] Joshua Speed stated that the United States had 180,000 to 200,000 slaves, and a military commander had issued an edict which declared 20,000 free in Kentucky. He wrote that the entire people of Kentucky out of necessity would have to resist, because the loyal slaveholder and the non slaveholder would be united in their resistance. In his opinion, cruelty and crime would rule the land and the black people would be exterminated in the state. According to Joshua Speed, the public sentiment was fixed against freeing blacks and allowing blacks to be emancipated and remain among the whites. He wrote to Lincoln that "you had as well attack the freedom of worship in the North or the right of a parent to teach his child to read—as to wage war in a slave state on such a principle."[131] He asked Lincoln to think hard on the subject.

Lincoln asked General Fremont to modify his order to official policy, under the Confiscation Act of 1861, which freed only those slaves used by the Confederates to aid the war effort, but did not extend to general abolition. Fremont refused. Lincoln could not alienate the border-states with such a radical move; neither could he ignore the Radical Republicans calling for abolition. Lincoln became alarmed over Fremont's proclamation which pronounced a death penalty for Confederate guerillas and confiscated the property and slaves of Confederate sympathizers. He also became aware of Fremont's military incompetence. On October 24, 1861, Lincoln removed Fremont from command and revoked his order.[132]

By the end of August, Confederate General Gideon Pillow tried to pressure Confederate General Leonidas Polk into allowing him to take Columbus, Kentucky. Polk adopted Pillow's idea as his own. For three months, Polk had collected information on Kentucky.

Columbus, Kentucky, a town situated on high bluffs overlooking the Mississippi River, represented a better position from which to defend Tennessee's stretch of river than any place in the northern part of the state. By the end of August 1861, rumors circulated in the South that Federal forces were also preparing to seize Columbus. The rumors were, in fact, true. On August 28, 1861, Union General John

130 Joshua Speed to Abraham Lincoln, September 3, 1861, The Abraham Lincoln Papers, The Library of Congress, Washington, D.C.

131 Ibid.

132 Patricia Faust, *Historical Times Illustrated Encyclopedia of the Civil War*, (New York: Harper & Row Publishers, 1986), 291.

Fremont had ordered Colonel Ulysses S. Grant to seize Columbus as soon as possible. Tennessee Governor Isham Harris informed Polk on September 2 to leave matters alone for a couple of days. Governor Isham Harris hoped that the Federals would invade Kentucky first and take Columbus. If the Yankees invaded Kentucky first, pro-Southern Kentuckians would then have the provocation they needed to take Kentucky out of the Union and into the Confederacy. Polk had other plans. Polk wrote to Governor Benjamin Magoffin of Kentucky that "it (is) of the greatest importance to the Southern cause in Kentucky or elsewhere that I should be ahead of the enemy in occupying Columbus and Paducah."[133] Back in Richmond, Virginia, Confederate President Jefferson Davis had no idea that Polk was planning to invade Kentucky and occupy Columbus. On September 2, 1861, Davis wrote to Polk: "Keep me better advised of your forces and purposes. It is only when forewarned that I can meet your wishes or your wants."[134] On September 3, 1861, Pillow, acting under Polk's orders, moved his troops into Kentucky and Columbus thereby violating Kentucky's neutrality.[135] On September 4, 1861 Harris learned that Polk had invaded the state. Harris telegraphed Polk: "Just learned that Pillow's command is at Hickman. This is unfortunate, as the President and myself are pledged to respect the neutrality of Kentucky. I hope they will be withdrawn instantly, unless their presence there is an absolute necessity."[136] As reprinted in the Official Records, on September 4, Secretary of War L.P. Walker telegraphed Polk: "News has reached me here that General Pillow has landed his troops at Hickman, Ky. Order their prompt withdrawal from Kentucky."[137] On September 4, Polk sent a telegram to Davis stating that the enemy had descended the Mississippi River and placed cannons and entrenched themselves opposite the town of Columbus, which Polk wrote "left no doubt upon the minds of any of their intention to seize and forcibly posses said town, I thought proper, under the plenary power delegated to

133 O. R. Series I, Vol. IV, Chapter XII. Sept. 3-12, 1861.--Advance of Confederate Forces into Kentucky; occupation of Columbus, etc., No. 1. Report of Maj. Gen. Leonidas Polk, C. S. Army, of the occupation of Columbus and Hickman, Ky., September 3, with correspondence and orders., 180.

134 Crist and Dix, ed., *The Papers of Jefferson Davis*, vol. 7, 318.

135 Woodworth, "The Indeterminate Quantities," 291: Steven Woodworth, *Jefferson Davis and his Generals: The Failure of Confederate High Command in the West* (Lawrence: University of Kansas, 1997), 38.

136 Ibid., 182.

137 Ibid.

me, to direct a sufficient portion of my command, both by river and by land, to concentrate at Columbus . . . It is my intention to continue to occupy and keep this position."[138] As reprinted in the Official Records, on September 4, this was Davis' response to Polk's invasion of Kentucky: "The necessity justifies the action."[139]

Because of Polk's invasion of Kentucky on September 3, 1861, the Union army had justification to enter Kentucky, did so, and seized Paducah, located on the mouth of the Tennessee River. The Federals had outflanked Columbus which held no military value to the Confederacy and the place became a trap. Columbus did not add any additional security against a Union advance. Holding Columbus would not prevent an invasion of Tennessee through the Tennessee and Cumberland Rivers. The town of Columbus was easily flanked and encircled by a movement against the Tennessee and Cumberland Rivers. As historian Thomas Connelly stated in the *Army of the Heartland,* Columbus was a weak position, but its occupation placed the West Tennessee defenses on an exterior line.[140]

After the invasion of Kentucky, the Union troops hoisted the stars and stripes above the capitol in Frankfort. On September 9, John M. Johnston sent Polk a message that the Senate of Kentucky had passed a resolution that the occupation of Hickman, Chalk Bank, and Columbus by Confederate troops had been taken with astonishment and that such an act was committed by Confederate forces. The Senate asked Polk to withdraw from Kentucky. Polk responded that it was "only perceived that continued indifference to our rights and our safety was about to culminate in the seizure of an important part of her territory by the United States forces for offensive operations against the United States that a regard for self preservation demanded of us to seize it in advance. We are here, therefore, not by choice, but by necessity."[141] Polk would only remove his troops, if the Federal government withdrew their troops. President Davis, Tennessee Governor Isham Harris, Kentucky Governor Beriah Magoffin, and Inspector General of the Kentucky State Guard Simon

138 Ibid.

139 Ibid.

140 Thomas Connelly, *Army of the Heartland-Army of Tennessee 1861-1862*, (Baton Rouge & London: Louisiana State University Press, 1967, reprint, 1983), 54.

141 O.R. series I, vol. IV, chapter XII., Sept. 3-12, 1861. Advance of Confederate Forces into Kentucky; occupation of Columbus, etc., 190.

Buckner, all asked Polk to leave. Jacob Thompson, from the Memphis Committee of Safety, pleaded with Davis that he appoint a general to take charge of all the military operations in the Mississippi Valley. The "universal voice of the people in every direction says, give us Johnson. The Soldiers cry out for God's sake give us Johnson. All the Generals will most cheerfully accept Johnson."[142]

On September 13, Davis changed his mind about the invasion of Kentucky that it had been the wrong decision, and wrote to Polk that his occupation of Columbus had been necessary as a defensive measure. The next day, Polk sent Davis a letter stating that the seizure of Kentucky was overrated in the public mind of Kentucky. As for the protection of Tennessee, the seizure of Kentucky was a military necessity. Polk wrote to Davis that he should have seized Columbus months ago. Kentucky "melted away under the influence of the Lincoln Government."[143] Polk stated that the Confederates must make a stand, and do it vigorously. Polk prophesied that more Confederate allies in Kentucky would rally to him if the Confederates would win a few battles. Kentucky would abandon the Federal government, once the fear of the Federal government's power that constrained Kentucky had been lifted. Polk pleaded with Davis to send more armies and more commanders. Polk wrote to Davis that the state of Kentucky "will rally strongly to our support for their emancipation."[144] Unfortunately Polk did not understand the true political nature of Kentucky. Because of the invasion of Kentucky, the people saw the Confederates as the aggressors, not the liberators.

Senator John Helm of Kentucky warned Polk that the invasion of Kentucky would inflame the public mind against the Confederate States, and the Kentucky legislature would inaugurate measures for the creation of a force to eject Polk out of the state. The Kentucky Legislature disbanded the Kentucky State Guard, under General Simon Buckner, and locked up the arms used by the Kentucky State Guard in the State Arsenal at Frankfort. Union General Robert Anderson began to raise a force of 30,000 men in Kentucky. Senator John Helm pointed out that Kentucky was still in the Union and the Confederate

142 Lynda Crist and Mary Dix, *The Papers of Jefferson Davis*, vol. 7, 1861, (Baton Rouge & London: Louisiana State University Press, 1993), 329.

143 O.R. series I, vol. IV, chapt. XII., Sept. 3-12, 1861.

144 O.R. series I, vol. IV, chapt. XII., Sept. 3-12, 1861, Advance of Confederate Forces into Kentucky; occupation of Columbus, etc., 192.

states were in rebellion. Polk had to leave the state first before the Union troops would leave the state.[145]

On September 13, 1861, the speaker of the Kentucky Senate John Fisk telegraphed Lincoln with a proposal to preserve Kentucky's neutrality by having Union and Confederate forces withdraw from the state.

By September 15, 1861, Davis had accepted Polk's explanation for the invasion of Kentucky. Davis wrote to Polk that Governor Harris and others had told him that the invasion of Kentucky would work political detriment to the Confederate cause in Kentucky. Davis admitted that it was true that the solution of the problem of Polk's invasion of Kentucky required the consideration of others, such as Kentucky's governor, and the legislators. But he stated that the Confederacy could not permit the indeterminate quantities, the political elements, to control the Confederate actions in cases of military necessity.[146] Davis wrote to Polk that Albert Sidney Johnston was on his way and would command operations in the West. Davis was glad that the people of Columbus saw Polk as the defender of their rights; unfortunately, Columbus was one of the few cities which did support the invasion of Kentucky.

On September 15, 1861, Confederate General Albert Sidney Johnston arrived in Nashville and took command of the Department of the West. Johnston assigned Polk the First Division, Western Department, which included Columbus and the upper Mississippi River defenses.

On September 17, Joshua Speed wrote to Lincoln that he had traveled to Frankfort. He stated that the Confederate sympathizers were strong enough to obstruct any bills by parliamentary tactics, but the Union men held firm. He wanted Lincoln to send more arms. He informed Lincoln that Union men could not go into camp without arms, as they could in the North, since pro-Confederate citizens lived in their state. Secretary of War Simon Cameron promised to send them. He asked Lincoln to make sure that General George Ramsey, commander of the Washington D. C., arsenal, shipped the ammunition and weapons to him.[147]

---

145 Ibid., 192.

146 Ibid., 195.

147 Joshua Speed to Abraham Lincoln, Sept. 17, 1861, The Abraham Lincoln Papers, The Library of Congress, Washington, D.C.

On that same day, General William T. Sherman crossed the river to Camp Joe Holt with the news that Confederate General Simon Buckner was approaching the city. Union Colonel Lovell Rousseau decided to take his troops to Louisville. The next day Rousseau marched his 11,200 men to Muldraugh Hill. On September 19, 1861, 1,500 Union men arrived in Lexington and camped on the fairgrounds. A few days later, 3,500 more Union troops arrived into town.

The next day, on September 18, 1861, Joshua Speed left for Washington, D.C., to procure more weapons for Unionists in Kentucky. After one week, he managed to secure 5,000 Springfield muskets from Boston, 5,000 Belgian rifles from New York, and hoped to get another 4,000 Springfield rifles in Pennsylvania.[148]

Many members of the Union Central Committee suspected that Kentucky Governor Beriah Magoffin sympathized with the Confederates. A Military Board of five men oversaw the military affairs in Kentucky. The secessionists plotted to reduce the power of the military board by proposing that no order would be effective unless the sanction received a vote of four-fifths of the military board members. James Speed stated that the proposition would nullify the action of the board since one member could control the action of the whole board. Speed made sure the proposal was rejected. The secessionists again tried to limit the power of the board by stating that the board issued no additional arms, but had confined themselves to equalizing those arms previously given out between the State and Home Guard. James Speed demonstrated there was no intention to disarm any portion of the state and that there was no law that existed which provided when companies might disband, nor was there a law to punish persons for a misapplication of the state arms. His only object for the arms was to keep them out of the hands of irresponsible parties.[149]

One of James Speed's first acts as Senator was to secure a resolution requesting the Governor to inform the Senate of the number of arms belonging to the state, their location, condition, the quantity of ammunition, the members and location of active and reserve militia, and the names of the field officers in command.[150]

On September 30, 1861, the Kentucky legislature passed an

---

148 Williams, "Joshua and James Speed: Lincoln's Kentucky Friends," 109.

149 Helen Springer, "The Political Career of James Speed," 48; Gary Lee Williams, "James and Joshua Speed: Lincoln's Kentucky Friends," 108.

150 Springer, "The Political Career of James Speed," 48.

act directing the Governor to call out 42,000 Kentuckians to repel the Confederate invasion. The Military Board reorganized and assumed complete control of military authority. The Board borrowed $1 million and voted a week later for another $2 million. Senator James Speed negotiated with the Farmer's Bank, Northern Bank of Kentucky, Bank of Kentucky, and the Bank of Louisville for the loans. The officials at the Bank of Louisville did not want to loan the money. James Speed introduced a resolution authorizing the Committee on banks to investigate the condition and management of the Bank of Louisville. The resolution passed the Senate and House. The entire state armament came under the control of the Military Board.[151]

James Speed supported a bill to compel the attendance of absent members of the Kentucky Legislature. Members of the Senate objected to the bill, stating it was "unnecessary, unconstitutional, and derogatory to the members of the Legislature in permitting them to be arrested by petty officers." Speed explained that the bill compelled the attendance of the legislature in order to safeguard the public peace and the security of the state. Speed stated that the people had the right to demand fulfillment of all the duties of their representatives. The bill passed the Senate and the House. Rumors circulated that Senator J.M. Johnson met with Confederate authorities. Speed introduced a resolution that a committee be appointed to investigate Senator Johnson. The Kentucky legislature appointed James Speed to the committee.[152]

On October 7, 1861, Joshua Speed wrote to Lincoln that General Robert Anderson had surrendered his command gracefully and agreed that his decision to step down was necessary due to ill health. Joshua Speed, Larz Anderson, and James Guthrie asked that General Henry Halleck take command in Kentucky, which would give Kentucky General Sherman in the field and at the head of the center column. General Anderson preferred General William T. Sherman. Joshua stated if they wished to save Kentucky for the Union, Kentucky's force should be increased to a point that would enable them to drive General Buckner out of the state and carry the war into Tennessee. Union forces would be greatly increased both in Southern Kentucky and Tennessee by the presence of an over-powering force. In his opinion, the forces obtained in southern Kentucky and

151 Ibid., 50.
152 Springer, 51-52.

Tennessee would be burning with a desire for revenge, and the troops would know the geography of the area. Confederate General Felix Zollicoffer's army in Tennessee tried to invade the Cumberland Mountains, but according to Joshua Speed, he was met with a "warm reception. . . . The advance of his army was so harassed by the mountain riflemen picking off his men—that he was forced to retreat."[153] He finished his letter stating that he hoped to visit Lincoln in Washington.

Before he left for Washington, Union General William T. Sherman paid Joshua Speed a visit and complained to him that Washington did not heed his requests for more men, ammunition, and arms. Speed asked, "What do you want?"

Sherman replied, "Everything. Arms, wagons, tents, bread and meat, money, and a competent staff." Speed told Sherman to write everything down on paper and give him the list. Sherman hastily wrote down his list and handed the paper to Joshua, who took the train to Washington and submitted the list to Lincoln.

While in Washington, Lincoln and Joshua discussed not only the war, but also of former days. During the conversation, Lincoln must have asked Joshua about his mother, Lucy Speed. Joshua Speed said: "Mother would like a picture of you." Lincoln took out a recent photograph of himself made by Mathew Brady, and inscribed on the photograph, "To Mrs. Lucy Speed, from whose pious hands I received an Oxford Bible twenty years ago. October 3, 1861."[154]

Upon his return from Washington, Joshua Speed paid Sherman a visit in his Louisville headquarters. He handed Sherman copies of orders naming two important officers in the quartermaster corps to be assigned to his staff, with a drawing account for $100,000. One order, signed by Lincoln, directed the ordnance department to supply the Kentucky forces with 10,000 Model 1861 Springfield rifled muskets. Sherman asked Joshua Speed, "How is this that more attention is paid to the requests of you, a citizen, than me, a general in the army? You had better take command here."

Quietly Speed told Sherman of his friendship with Lincoln and then said: "The only mistake you made, General, was not asking for more."[155]

---

153 Joshua Speed to Abraham Lincoln, October 7, 1861, The Abraham Lincoln Papers, The Library of Congress, Washington, D.C.

154 Robert Kincaid, *Joshua Speed: Lincoln's Most Intimate Friend*, 26.

155 Ibid., 25-26.

Joshua Speed's acquisition of weapons for General Sherman and the Home Guard did not go unnoticed. A Louisville correspondent for the *New York Times* paid Joshua Speed a tribute by writing that the arms secured for Kentucky were mainly procured by Joshua Speed and that Kentucky owned him a "great debt of gratitude for his untiring exertions on his behalf."[156] The correspondent went on to describe Joshua F. Speed as a "modest, retiring, unassuming man; but his great practical wisdom is known here to his friends. He is a man of large, comprehensible, practical common sense, and this is the substratum of his greatness. He is unquestionably a man of great wisdom. . . . He is a man of true virtues, the purest honor, and the most incorruptible integrity." The correspondent pointed out that James Guthrie, who was Joshua Speed's neighbor and friend, appreciated Joshua Speed and held the same opinion as the correspondent. The reporter told his readers that "It is fortunate for Kentucky that Mr. Lincoln knows and appreciates Mr. Speed. . . . I esteem it fortunate for Kentucky, in this hour of peril, that one of her sons is known to the head of the Federal government to be a prudent and wise man, worthy of all confidence. Mr. Speed has rendered the State great service, and will ever be ready to devote himself to the cause of the State and the Government."[157]

By late October James Speed became concerned with all the young men of Kentucky joining the Confederacy and how Kentucky's young men literally fought brother against brother. He wrote: "So many of our giddy young men have gone into the Southern army that almost every man who goes into our army, knows that he has to fight a neighbor, a relative, a brother, son or father—I have been astonished to find how many persons permit family ties to override their allegiance to the government."[158]

On November 5, 1861, President Lincoln wrote to James Guthrie and James Speed inquiring about how close Confederate General Simon Buckner's forces were to Louisville. Buckner had set up his headquarters in Bowling Green, Kentucky. Lincoln asked if Buckner had crossed the Green River, or whether the Green River Bridge had been repaired, and whether Buckner could cross the Green River in front of Union General Alexander McCook's forces. He asked how

156 *The Louisville Daily Journal*, October 16, 1861.

157 Ibid.

158 Coulter, *The Civil War and Readjustment in Kentucky*, 119.

long McCook could hold off Buckner's forces if they approached Louisville. Lincoln received a telegram stating that if General Sherman was not reinforced, he would meet the same fate as General Nathaniel Lyon in Missouri. George Prentice sent Lincoln a telegram stating that Buckner's forces were six or seven times Sherman's size.[159]

Little did James Speed and James Guthrie know, but Sherman had asked to be relieved of command. Union General Don Carlos Buell became the new commander for Kentucky. On that same day, Simon Cameron, Secretary of War, asked that Lincoln stop Joshua Speed from buying or attempting to buy arms. Cameron stated that the result of his efforts to buy weapons would enhance the price of weapons and defeat the efforts of the government to procure arms. Cameron stated that in a few days, enough arms would supply Joshua Speed's demands and save the government a great expense. Lincoln did not order Joshua Speed to stop procuring arms and Joshua Speed continued in his efforts to buy weapons for Kentucky Unionists.[160]

On November 11, 1861, Joshua Speed and T.S. Bell wrote to Lincoln recommending Joseph Holt to a position on Lincoln's cabinet. Joseph Holt was born in Breckinridge City, Kentucky, in 1807 and educated at St. Joseph's and Centre Colleges. He practiced law in Elizabethtown, Kentucky, moved to Louisville, and then to Port Gibson, Mississippi. He returned to Louisville as a lawyer. In 1856, he supported James Buchanan and was appointed commissioner of patents, postmaster general, and secretary of war. Joshua Speed and T.S. Bell stated that the rebellion wrecked Joseph Holt's private resources. They asked President Lincoln to appoint Holt to a position worthy of his "unselfish loyalty, his rare abilities, his energies, and fidelity."[161] Joshua and Bell testified that as a lawyer, Holt was "scarcely surpassed in this country." He wrote that Joseph Holt was "one of the cherished jewels of our State pride, and if you seek out a place suitable for such a man as he has proved himself to be and put him in it, you will make Kentucky love you yet more than she does."[162] Lincoln appointed Holt judge advocate general of the army with the rank of colonel.

159 Basler, *Collected Works of Abraham Lincoln*, Volume 5, Lincoln to James Guthrie and James Speed, Nov. 5, 1861., 15.

160 Simon Cameron to Abraham Lincoln, Nov. 5, 1861, The Abraham Lincoln Papers, The Library of Congress, Washington, D.C.

161 Joshua Speed and T. S. Bell to Abraham Lincoln, Nov. 11, 1861, The Abraham Lincoln Papers, The Library of Congress, Washington, D.C.

162 Ibid.

James Guthrie wrote to Joshua Speed about the military affairs in Kentucky, which he passed on to Lincoln's desk. Guthrie wrote that the Union men of the state wanted General Sherman to stay in Kentucky and lead the advance against the Confederates. Guthrie did not support General Alexander McCook, because his manners did warrant the position of commanding general. In Guthrie's opinion, McCook could command a brigade of five or six regiments better than any general in Kentucky. Guthrie wrote to Joshua Speed that Kentucky wanted more brigadier generals of the best military schools. Generals Jeremiah Boyle, William T. Ward, James Negley, Lovell Rousseau, and Thomas Crittenden were all good men, but not yet first rate generals, and these generals must be with the brigades in the advance. Guthrie asked why the government could not spare Kentucky five or six educated and practicable warriors for brigadier generals. Guthrie pointed out that if Kentucky could field 100,000 men, they must have 24 brigadier generals, but at present the state only had six who were educated and practical soldiers, and one of them was already a commanding general. Guthrie also stated that if their colonels and subordinate officers were educated practical soldiers, Kentucky could better dispense with experienced brigadier generals. Lincoln endorsed the letter and asked if Union General George McClellan could appoint Don Carlos Buell a Major General, allowing Sherman to return to Kentucky. Lincoln stated that Buell agreed with Guthrie that about half a dozen more brigadier generals were needed in Kentucky.[163]

Guthrie felt that the reason Union General Sherman joined Union General Henry Halleck in Saint Louis was for the purpose of a combined movement by the Mississippi from Cairo, Illinois, and Paducah, Kentucky, and from there push into middle Tennessee. Guthrie felt the plan of using Cairo and Paducah as a launching site for the Federal armies was the right way to move forward. He feared that military strategists in Washington preferred an invasion of east Tennessee by the Cumberland Gap. By implementing this plan, Confederate Generals Leonidas Polk, Albert Sidney Johnston and Simon Buckner would be able to occupy their present position on the southern and western borders of the state and threaten the whole Ohio

163 James Guthrie to Joshua Speed, Nov. 22, 1861, endorsement by Lincoln, Nov. 27, 1861, The Abraham Lincoln papers, The Library of Congress, Washington, D.C.

border for the next six months. The result would devastate the Union cause in the southern and western counties of Kentucky.[164]

Guthrie stated in his letter that the Federal armies must advance by the Mississippi River aided by an advance through middle Tennessee from Kentucky on the line through Bowling Green, Kentucky. He stated that if the Federal move came through Virginia to Richmond, fortified camps and mountain passes and disciplined troops would faced the oncoming Federals, costing many lives and money. Even if the Federal troops took Richmond, the main work had just begun, because mountain passes with fortified camps and disciplined forces would drive back only by force, and the Federal army would have to protect their base line with many troops and transport many supplies at a great expense.[165]

But if the Federal troops advanced down the Mississippi River and through Tennessee, the Federal army would encounter no fortified camps, no defensible mountains, and comparatively speaking, no disciplined troops. They would have cheap lines of transportation and when the army reached New Orleans, the heart of the Confederacy would have been destroyed. Guthrie felt that the great battle was to be fought in Kentucky, not the Potomac or on the Atlantic shores. He also felt that the enemy should be fought at all points, giving the enemy no rest, but making haste slowly. In Guthrie's opinion, a winter campaign must be made and no winter quarters taken by the Federal army. Confident in his opinion, Guthrie believed the Federal army could take Nashville before Christmas and that the occupation of east Tennessee would be freed from the Confederate oppressors.[166]

In his letter, Guthrie mentioned that Secretary of War Simon Cameron recommended Union General John Cochran's speech implementing the use of former slaves as soldiers. Guthrie disagreed with using black soldiers. He wrote: "The Union can be restored by white soldiers without arming the blacks, and nineteen millions of white men should have more manhood than to call in the aid of negroes to subdue six millions of whites weakened by the presence of

164 James Guthrie to Joshua Speed, Nov. 22, 1861, endorsed by Speed Nov. 26, 1861; endorsed by Lincoln Nov. 26, 1861, The Abraham Lincoln Papers, The Library of Congress, Washington, D.C.

165 Ibid.

166 Ibid.

four million of slaves."[167] Guthrie's mood did not differ from many Kentuckians, especially the slave owners. In Secretary of War Cameron's annual report, he advocated the arming of former slaves. Cameron released the report to the press. In the *Louisville Journal*, editor George Prentice stated that Lincoln favored the "Cameron" doctrine and spoke for the loyal men of Louisville. Prentice counseled Kentucky Union officers to resign. Lincoln made Cameron eliminate the portion of recruiting and arming former slaves as soldiers from the report before he submitted the report to Congress.[168] Lincoln had not introduced the Emancipation Proclamation yet, and many Kentuckians did not favor the use of former slaves as soldiers.

Joshua Speed endorsed Guthrie's letter and added that the Louisville & Nashville Railroad would be the "column advancing along its line, what a gangway is to a steam boat, reaching the shore of the Northwest from which you have to draw your supplies of men and provisions." He suggested that the chief cost of the railroad was the grade. If the Confederates retreated, they would tear up the rail, but the grade remained. The Nashville Road cost $42,000 per mile to build, the grade costing $32,000 per mile and the iron rails a mere $10,000 per mile. Joshua stated that the Green River Bridge, destroyed by the Confederates at Bowling Green, could be repaired in a couple of days at a cost of $40,000 and that the Louisville & Nashville Railroad Company was ready to advance and repair as the army advanced. Joshua Speed pointed out that every county along the line from Louisville to Nashville was Union and would protect the road in the rear of the army as the army advanced. He also stated that Middle Tennessee had fertile soil and grew a large amount of cotton. As the Union army advanced, commerce would be developed along the way.[169] President Lincoln read the letter and wrote that Union General George McClellan should see the letter.

On December 22, 1861, James Speed wrote to Lincoln about the affairs in Frankfort. He stated that the legislature should keep a watch on Governor Beriah Magoffin for the remainder of his term. James Speed felt that Magoffin was a Rebel at heart and "afflicted beyond

167 Ibid.

168 T. S. Bell to Abraham Lincoln, December 6, 1861, The Abraham Lincoln Papers, The Library of Congress, Washington, D.C.

169 James Guthrie to Joshua Speed, Nov. 22, 1861, endorsed by Speed Nov. 26, 1861; endorsed by Lincoln Nov. 26, 1861, The Abraham Lincoln Papers, The Library of Congress, Washington, D.C.

hope of a cure." James Speed felt that the Governor did not even recognize that there was a rebellion in the state or that there was a rebel governor. On November 18 through 20, 1861, Confederate supporters met in Russellville, Kentucky, to set up a "Provisional Confederate Government of Kentucky" and elected George W. Johnson as the Confederate Governor. James Speed wrote to Lincoln that Governor Magoffin embarrassed the legislature and that the Governor hoped for the success of the rebellion. Magoffin harassed the legislature, but James Speed felt the Kentucky legislature could control the governor, unless the Union army faced defeat and the state was overrun.

James Speed wrote to Lincoln that he introduced a bill in the Senate legislation confiscating the estates belonging to Rebels. He thought that the bill would have gained more support if some other member of the Senate had introduced it, but the Senate regarded him as an abolitionist, and anything he suggested on the subject of slavery was regarded with suspicion. When the legislature met again, James was going to introduce the bill again. His bill provided that confiscated slaves would be reported to the state and disposed of from time to time. In explaining the bill to a caucus, members asked him why he did not provide for the sale of slaves as of other property. James Speed replied that he would not vote for the sale of a slave belonging to the state, that the state should never sell a human being by his vote. His comment produced a lot of excitement among the caucus members and prejudiced the prospects of passing the bill. James Speed thought that Lincoln should understand how Kentuckian politicians felt about the subject of slavery. He wrote that politicians "desire to please and not to offend their constituents; they lose all individuality of character, and it never seems to occur to them that their constituents are intelligent, honest, and content that justice and right shall be done. Such controlling feelings make legislators timid about interfering with the relation of master and slave."[170] James Speed did not want Lincoln to think that the pro-slavery feeling in the state controlled the legislature. He felt that the Kentuckians grew to hate southern traitors and had a "warm affection for the loyal citizens of the North."[171]

---

170 James Speed to Abraham Lincoln, Dec. 22, 1861, The Abraham Lincoln Papers, The Library of Congress, Washington, D.C.

171 Ibid.

James wrote that the institution of slavery must obey the great laws of economy. The war was the beginning of the institution's end. Slaves would lose their value. Masters would set slaves free when they ceased to be valuable. In his opinion, the emancipation feeling in Kentucky rose and fell with the rise and fall in the price of slaves. Particular individuals acted independently of the great laws of economy that produced the result, but communities never had and never would. On December 3, 1861, Lincoln gave his annual message to Congress, and the *Louisville Journal* accused him of supporting Simon Cameron's doctrine of arming slaves against the Confederacy. The paper asked for Union officers to resign. James Speed wanted Lincoln to know that the *Louisville Journal*'s comments had no effect on the legislature, but he feared the paper had a bad effect on the people. The southern supporters encouraged guerilla warfare. James Speed felt that Cameron exhibited the common weakness of "talking in advance of action—Solomon says there is a time for all things. This is a time for action, not for words—Many who condemn Mr. Cameron for what he said, would approve the conduct he invites when the case arises for it."[172]

As 1861 came to a close, Joshua and James Speed helped Lincoln in securing Kentucky in loyal Union hands. Joshua and James Speed also managed to secure valuable arms and ammunition for the Unionists and the newly forming Union regiments. Although Confederate troops took Bowling Green, Cumberland Gap, and Columbus, Kentucky, Louisville and Frankfort remained in Union control. Lincoln worried that Kentucky might fall into Confederate hands, but with the help of Unionists such as Joshua and James Speed, his fears of a Confederate Kentucky faded from his mind. As 1862 arrived, Joshua and James Speed continued to work to keep Lincoln informed about the conditions in Kentucky. James became more radical in his views toward Confederate sympathizers and passed laws limiting their freedoms. Joshua continued to secure arms and ammunition for the Union troops.

172 Ibid.

Chapter Eight

Grant Takes Control in the West

By January 1862, Confederate forces controlled the eastern half of Kentucky in the Cumberland Gap area, Columbus, Kentucky in western Kentucky, and Bowling Green, Kentucky, on the vital Louisville and Nashville Railroad. Union forces gathered in Missouri and Louisville. By late January, Union forces under General George Thomas defeated Confederate General Felix Zollicoffer at the Battle of Mill Springs, and by February 1862, Union forces under General Ulysses S. Grant defeated Confederate General Lloyd Tilghman at Fort Henry and Confederate General Simon Bolivar Buckner at Fort Donelson. Confederate General Albert Sidney Johnston had no choice but to leave Kentucky. Lincoln, Joshua and James Speed breathed a sigh of relief as the Confederate forces left, but another invading force under Confederate General Braxton Bragg entered Kentucky in August of 1862, again threatening the state. As a senator, James Speed continued in his efforts to secure Kentucky for the Union, implementing radical laws to punish disloyal citizens. In July 1862, Lincoln asked Joshua and James Speed's opinion on the Emancipation Proclamation. Both thought the proclamation was a bad idea. For the first time, Lincoln did not heed the advice from his friends in Kentucky, and decided to push his emancipation proclamation.

By December 1861, Johnston focused his attention on the Bowling Green, Kentucky, line while he neglected other areas. Confederate Colonel Thomas Heiman warned Confederate General Leonidas Polk to reinforce Fort Henry and Fort Donelson. By January 1862, the warning produced little results. Fort Henry was prone to flooding and had not even been relocated to higher ground. Construction began on Fort Heiman, located on higher ground, but the fort never saw completion. The neglect of the river defenses on the Cumberland and Tennessee Rivers was a direct result from Polk's neglect. He knew about the weak condition of the forts from Confederate

General Lloyd Tilghman, who was commander of the forts, but Columbus obsessed him.

Confederate General Albert Sidney Johnston ordered Confederate engineers to be sent to Forts Henry and Donelson, but Polk chose to ignore Johnston and delayed the departure of the engineers. He told Johnston that Lieutenant Joseph Dixon and the other engineers could not be spared. Johnston had to issue two additional orders to Polk before Dixon left to visit the forts. Polk did not volunteer any troops to the inland forts during the fall of 1861. Johnston commanded Polk to send four companies of infantry to guard the Danville, Tennessee, bridge, where the Memphis, Clarksville, and Louisville Railroad crossed the Tennessee River.[173]

Polk ordered General Lloyd Tilghman to complete the works, place its armaments, and use the surrounding labor to help in his task. General Albert Sidney Johnston wrote that the forts up to that point had been grossly managed. The officer in charge of the batteries was frequently absent, and the commander of Fort Donelson was away from his post nightly. Johnston requested that Governor Harris of Tennessee send four additional armed companies to the forts. Once those companies arrived they would be joined with the other six companies already there to form a regiment. Tilghman was to report to Confederate General Leonidas Polk monthly. Forts Henry and Donelson fell under Polk's jurisdiction.[174]

General Tilghman pointed out to Polk that both forts where in horrible shape and were not ready for battle. Tilghman requested more heavy guns for both Forts, four for each Fort and one to be long ranged, such as 64-pounders. Tilghman also had 1,000 unarmed men. Tilghman pleaded with Polk to send him more troops, field artillery, and supplies. Polk sent nothing. Tilghman wrote in a letter to Colonel W.W. Mackall that he was discouraged but would not give up.[175]

Despite the poor conditions at the forts, communication between Johnston, Tilghman, and Polk broke down. Johnston never knew that the forts were in a defenseless condition because Polk never

173 Thomas Connelly, *Army of the Heartland-Army of the Tennessee, 1861-1862*, (Baton Rouge & London: Louisiana State University Press, 1967, reprint 1983), 83.

174 O.R. Series I, vol. IV, chapt. XII, Correspondence, Orders, And Returns Relating Specially To Operations In Kentucky And Tennessee From July 1 To November 19, 1861. Confederate Correspondence, etc, 456.

175 Bush, *The Civil War Battles of the Western Theater*, 53.

volunteered any information about the condition of the forts. By the end of 1861, the breakdown in the Confederate command structure left the inland river defenses the most vulnerable area on the Tennessee border.[176]

In January 1862, Polk had the strongest force in the area. He had 21,000 men and 150 cannon at Columbus. He did not use his force to bolster the defenses at Forts Henry and Donelson. He told Johnston that any Federal force aimed at any point in his district other than Columbus would have to be the responsibility of the War Department and the people in the area. During the month of January, Johnston made no effort to force Polk to defend the eastern part of his district.[177]

In January 1861, the first part of Johnston's defensive line began to crumble. During the Battle of Mill Springs, Kentucky, on January 19, 1862, Union General Speed Fry killed Confederate General Felix Zollicoffer and the Union force defeated the Confederates. The eastern half of Johnston's defensive line collapsed. In February 1862, Union General Ulysses Grant began an assault on Fort Henry. General Tilghman knew that Fort Henry was impossible to defend since most of the fort was under water, so he sent most of his infantry to Fort Donelson. More than fall back to Fort Donelson to command the remaining forces, he decided to personally command the batteries at Fort Henry. Grant's gunboats battled with the fort, and after most of the heavy Confederate artillery had been silenced, Tilghman surrendered. On February 13, 1862, Grant, along with his gunboats and infantry, assaulted Fort Donelson. The gunboats did not defeat the Confederates within the fort, but Grant's infantry surrounded the fort. On February 16, the Confederates came close to escaping, but because of a confused command structure and inefficient Confederate officers, such as Confederate Generals Gideon Pillow and John Floyd, Grant captured Fort Donelson.

Even when Union forces attacked Forts Henry and Fort Donelson, Polk refused to send troops. On February 5, he sent two infantry regiments and four cavalry regiments to move toward the Tennessee River, but the gesture came too late. As soon as word reached Johnston that the forts had fallen, he made plans to evacuate Bowling Green and fall back to Nashville, Tennessee. On February 4,

176 Connelly, *Army of the Tennessee*, 85.

177 Ibid., 106-108.

Confederate General P.G.T. Beauregard reported to Bowling Green to take command of the left wing at Columbus. On February 12, Beauregard reminded Johnston that Fort Henry's surrender endangered Columbus, which was now vulnerable to a flank attack. Beauregard recommended that Columbus be evacuated. Three days later, Johnston gave his approval for the evacuation.[178]

When Johnston arrived in Nashville, he discovered that the Confederates had not built any fortifications around the city and the supply service had totally collapsed. Johnston felt that he had no choice but to abandon Nashville and continue to fall back. Polk had invested so much time, energy, and resources at Columbus, he did not want to leave his "Gibraltar of the West." On February 16, Polk wrote to his wife that she should evacuate to his brother Lucius' place in Tennessee. He told her that he had sent troops to Paducah, under the command of General Benjamin Cheatham for the purpose of stopping reinforcements that were heading for Fort Donelson. General Johnston countermanded the order.

On March 2, 1862, Beauregard ordered Polk to evacuate Columbus and fall back to Memphis, Tennessee. After the fall of Columbus, the Confederate forts along the Mississippi began to crumble. Between March 3 through 14, 1862, New Madrid came under siege and finally fell on April 7, 1862. Also on April 7, 1862, Island No. 10 fell, and then on June 2, 1862, Memphis fell before the Union advance.

After the fall of Forts Henry and Donelson and the evacuation of Nashville, the scattered remnants of the Confederate army fell back to Corinth, Mississippi. General Albert Sidney Johnston demanded an explanation from Polk as to why Fort Henry and Donelson had fallen to Union forces. The fall of Fort Henry and Donelson was not only a humiliating situation for Polk; it was also a huge disaster for the Confederacy.

In February of 1862, James Speed's committee to investigate disloyal senators compiled affidavits and resolutions against Senators John M. Johnson and William T. Anthony and both were expelled. Senator Public Printer also came under James Speed's scrutiny and his committee began an investigation into Printer's loyalty and conduct. Speed supported the severest laws for the punishment of Kentuckians found guilty of complicity with the Confederacy.

178 Connelly, *Army of the Tennessee*, 132-136.

In the spring of 1862, James Speed advocated a bill declaring that complicity with rebellion would lead to expatriation. The bill had no provision for trial or judicial investigation of the offense.[179] James Speed favored a bill to "provide that all connected with educational institutions shall take the oath of allegiance." The legislature defeated the recommendation of the bill. Speed also wanted ministers to take the oath of allegiance before administering the rite of marriage, but an executive veto stopped the bill from passage. The bill contained a retroactive feature that if the minister had been guilty of disloyalty in the past, he should be deprived of his citizenship. The Senate passed the bill after the retroactive clause was removed.[180] As a member of the Committee of the Judiciary, Speed tried to control seditious speech.[181] He supported a bill in the Senate to provide for a state force of 10,000 men. The bill gave the governor power to appoint a brigadier general. Speed explained that the bill was not to form a militia, but to organize a State force or army. Speed proposed a substitute bill, which passed unanimously by the Senate. The substitute bill provided for the re-enactment of the State Guard law, with amendments and for the organization of the militia of the State. The Senate gave the governor power to call into state service all, or any portion of the militia.[182]

In April of 1862, Confederate forces under General Albert Sidney Johnston fought Union forces under General Ulysses S. Grant at Pittsburg Landing, Tennessee. On the first day of fighting a bullet hit General Albert Sidney Johnston's leg, severing an artery, leading to Johnston's death. Confederate General P.G.T. Beauregard took command of the army. On the second day's fighting, Union General Ulysses S. Grant's forces forced the Confederates from the field, resulting in a Union victory. During the spring and the beginning of the summer, Union forces pushed into Alabama. For a time Kentucky was no longer under a threat of Confederate invasion, but that was soon to change.

On July 14, 1862, Lincoln convened a special invitation to the representatives and senators from the border states at the

179 Helen Springer, "The Political Career of James Speed," (M.A. Thesis, University of Chicago, 1936), 52.

180 Helen Springer, 53-54.

181 Jennifer Cole, "Semper Eadem: An Interpretation of the Life and Career of James Speed," (M.A. Thesis, University of Louisville, 2003), 33.

182 Helen Springer, 55-56.

Executive Mansion. He asked how the senators from the border states felt about compensated emancipation. Charles Wickliffe, Garrett Davis, and John Crittenden from Kentucky responded with their opinion that emancipation interfered with states rights, was unconstitutional, the financial burden too great, and there were no funds to carry the plan into effect. Joshua Speed discussed the proposed Emancipation Proclamation with Lincoln. He knew that many Unionists in Kentucky with pro-slavery views would reject his proposal, and he advised the President against issuing the proclamation. Lincoln patiently outlined the arguments and felt that Speed "should see the harvest of good" which would come from the proclamation. He reminded Speed of a conversation with him more than 20 years ago when he was in a period of deep depression. At that time he said he "had done nothing to make any human being remember that he had lived," and that his desire was to link his name with some important event in the interest of his fellow man. He told Joshua Speed that the Emancipation Proclamation would fulfill his hope that his name would be linked with this important event.[183]

On July 28, 1862, James Speed wrote to Lincoln about the situation in Kentucky. He reported that the state was "swarming like a hive of bees—a terrible neighborhood warfare is the most likely result—It may not exist in the State generally, but it looks now very like it." The legislature tried to pass a draft law that would force men to take sides in the conflict. He stated that the draft would drive many to the South or into guerilla warfare or into the Union army. In the matter of the emancipation of blacks, James reported that some intelligent and influential men from various parts of the state were with the government no matter what would be done with or about blacks. He wrote to Lincoln that matters in the state were at best chaotic and that few men knew what to think or do the next day. Refugees from all parts of the state filled the city of Louisville, and various and confusing reports frightened many of them. He informed Lincoln that Union General Jeremiah Boyle, district military commander for Kentucky, remained faithful and true no matter what was said or done about the black people. James Speed reported that many men in the state were in a "wild frenzy."

183 Robert Kincaid, *Joshua Speed: Lincoln's Most Intimate Friend*, (Harrogate, Tennessee: Lincoln Memorial University, 1943), 27; Helen Springer, "The Political Career of James Speed," 62-64.

James pondered over Lincoln's emancipation proclamation. Lincoln had read the draft to James Speed, but he thought the proclamation would not do any good and would most probably do harm. He believed that the black man could not be emancipated by proclamation: "If the white man does not liberate him under the operation of the laws of political economy, he must share in the dangers that are to be encountered in his liberation—Let the negro be no party to the force which is applied for his liberation, [for] as soon as that force is withdrawn he would sink into slavery again. If he has not the spirit to strike for freedom, he has not the pride of character to make him keep it when [it is] given to him. It seems to me that commanders should have full authority to make such use of them as the exigencies of the service demands. A sweeping proclamation would be idle because impracticable. It would but delude the poor negro, and shock most violently the prejudice of many in the north and nearly all in the south."[184] He begged Lincoln to banish his idea that the black man could be set free or benefit from paper proclamations. He stated that the black man must strike for his own freedom.[185] To James Speed, slavery was a state issue, not a Federal issue.

On July 31, 1862, Confederate General Braxton Bragg and Major General Edmund Kirby Smith met in Chattanooga, Tennessee, to plan their invasion of Kentucky. Both generals were hoping to bring Kentucky into the fold of the Confederacy. Braxton Bragg had high hopes for Kentucky. Kentucky Confederate Calvary General John Hunt Morgan promised that Bragg would be able to pick up 100,000 men if he entered this state. Bragg was also looking for badly needed supplies. On August 13, 1862, Smith marched out of Knoxville with 9,000 men to Barbourville, Kentucky. On August 20, 1862, Smith announced that he would take Lexington. On August 28, 1862, Bragg's army moved toward Kentucky. At the Battle of Richmond, on August 30, Smith's Confederate forces defeated Union General William "Bull" Nelson's Union troops, capturing the entire force, essentially leaving Kentucky with no Union support. Nelson managed to escape back to Louisville. Smith marched into Lexington and sent a Confederate cavalry force to take Frankfort, Kentucky's capitol.

Union General Don Carlos Buell's army withdrew from Ala-

---

184 James Speed to Abraham Lincoln, July 28, 1862, The Abraham Lincoln Papers, The Library of Congress, Washington, D.C.

185 Ibid.

bama and headed back to Kentucky. Union General Henry Halleck, commander of all Union forces in the West, sent two divisions from General Ulysses Grant's army, stationed in Mississippi, to Buell. Morgan managed to destroy the Louisville & Nashville Railroad tunnel at Gallatin, Tennessee, cutting off all supplies to Buell's Union army. On September 3, Kentucky Governor James F. Robinson sent James Speed, Speaker of the House Richard Buckner, and Kentucky House of Representatives member John Houston to Washington, D.C., as special commissioners. On September 5, Buell reached Murfreesboro, Tennessee, and headed for Nashville, Tennessee. On September 6, the special commissioners from Kentucky, Ohio, Indiana and Illinois discussed the condition of military affairs in the West and especially of their conditions in Kentucky with Lincoln. Joshua Speed attended the committee meeting. Senator Lane opened for Indiana, Garrett Davis for Kentucky, and other gentlemen from Ohio and Illinois addressed Lincoln. They all had complaints about how the war was being waged in the West. President Lincoln sat on a revolving chair, looking at everyone until each man had his say. Lincoln said: "Now, gentlemen, I am going to make you a curious kind of speech. I announce to you that I am not going to do one single thing that any one of you has asked me to do. But it is due to myself and to you that I should give my reasons." From his seat, Lincoln answered each man, taking them in order in which they spoke, never forgetting a point that any one had made. When he was done, he rose from his chair and said: "Judge List, this reminds me of an anecdote which I heard a son of yours tell in Burlington, Iowa. He was trying to enforce upon his hearers the truth of the old adage that three moves is worse than fire. As an illustration he gave an account of a family who started from Western Pennsylvania pretty well off in this world's goods when they started. But they moved and moved, having less and less every time they moved, till after a while they could carry every thing in one wagon. He said that the chickens of the family got so used to being moved, that wherever they saw the wagon sheets brought out they laid themselves on their backs and crossed their legs, ready to be tied. Now, gentlemen, if I were to listen to every committee that comes in at that door, I had just as well as cross my hands and let you tie me. Nevertheless, I am glad to see you."[186]

186 Joshua Speed, *Reminiscences of Abraham Lincoln and Notes of a Visit to California*, (Bradley & Gilbert Co., 1896), 30.

On September 14, 1862, Confederate General Bragg reached Glasgow, Kentucky. On that same day, Union General Don Carlos Buell reached Bowling Green, Kentucky. Bragg decided to take Louisville. One of the major objectives of the Confederate campaign in Kentucky was to seize the Louisville and Portland Canal, severing Union supply routes on the Ohio River. One Confederate officer suggested destroying the Louisville canal so completely that "future travelers would hardly know where it was." On September 16, 1862, Bragg's army reached Munfordville, Kentucky. Confederate Colonel James Chalmers attacked the Federal garrison at Munfordville, but he was in over his head and Bragg had to bail him out. Bragg arrived at Munfordville with his entire force and the Union force at Munfordville surrendered. Buell left Bowling Green and headed for Louisville, Kentucky. Fearing that Buell would not arrive in Louisville to prevent Bragg's army from capturing the city, Union General William Nelson ordered the construction of a hasty defensive line around the city and the placement of pontoon bridges across the Ohio to facilitate the evacuation of the city or to receive reinforcements from Indiana. Two pontoon bridges, built of coal barges, one below the Big Four Bridge and the other from Portland to New Albany, were erected, but the Union army arrived to prevent the Confederate's seizure of the city.

On September 17, 1862, Joshua Speed wrote to Lincoln about the affairs in Kentucky, especially concerning Union General Jeremiah Boyle, military district commander for Kentucky. During the month of June and July, Boyle initiated a campaign of arrests. Anyone who gave aid to the Confederacy were ordered to turn themselves over to the provost marshals, to take an oath of allegiance, and to post bonds as security for future good conduct. Mass arrests occurred weekly. The Unionists in Kentucky recognized that Boyle's behavior threatened to destroy the Union cause. In mid-August, Secretary of War Edwin Stanton ordered General Boyle to stop making arrests on a mass scale and to arrest on with caution and good cause. At first Boyle complied with Stanton's request, but his subordinates continued in their arrests and Boyle did nothing to stop them.[187] Joshua Speed wrote to Lincoln that General Boyle had injured the government by his course of action. He said that he had told General Boyle

187 E. Merton Coulter, *The Civil War and Readjustment in Kentucky*, (Chapel Hill: University of North Carolina Press, 1921, reprint Glouster, Mass, 1966), 145-149.

that he injured the government, but Boyle persisted in his actions. In Boyle's first proclamation he announced that no man should be arrested on account of political opinions, that all men who remained at home attending to their business should be protected. In violation of his pledge, citizens had been arrested on no charges. They had been imprisoned without cause and turned out, not knowing and their friends not knowing, why they were arrested. Bayonets kept down armed opposition. Joshua Speed reported that provost marshals had been using their power for personal gain, levying black mail for administering the oath, but none of the provost marshals had been punished. At the time of Boyle's appointment, Boyle told Lincoln that in all matters of public interests, he would be advised by Joshua Speed, James Speed, and James Guthrie. Joshua Speed stated he differed with General Boyle and that General Boyle was a "good man, but in the wrong place."[188] He wrote to Lincoln that Boyle had imprisoned the jailor because he would not release the blacks in jail to his order. He explained to Lincoln that the Kentucky jails in all the counties in the state were used to hold turbulent and bad men, both black and white. If they were released at the dictation of every general as the army progressed, "the number will be very limited who will desire it to advance much farther in the state. The infernal negro cuts no figure in the case. But the subversion of local and state laws does."[189] He advised Lincoln that in the matters of arrest, Governor James F. Robinson should take command.[190]

Boyle denied that numerous arrests had been made, except during the period when a Confederate force was threatening in eastern Kentucky in Richmond. He stated that the charges made against him came from "weak-backed Union men, who hope to so act as to secure rebel protection."[191]

Although Lincoln asked for James and Joshua's opinion on his Emancipation Proclamation, he thought neither man saw the greater good. On September 22, 1862, Lincoln issued his preliminary Emancipation Proclamation. Joshua and James had correctly surmised the backlash that would occur if the Emancipation Proclamation was issued to the nation. Kentucky had to deal with a Confederate

---

188 Joshua Speed to Abraham Lincoln, Sept. 17, 1862, The Abraham Lincoln Papers, The Library of Congress, Washington, D.C.

189 Ibid.

190 Ibid.

191 O.R. Series I, vol. 16, Part 2, 519.

invasion first, but once Lincoln's Emancipation Proclamation sank in, the state cried out against it.

On September 25, 1862, Buell's tired and hungry men arrived in Louisville. Bragg moved his army to Bardstown, but did not take Louisville. Bragg urged General Smith to join his forces to take Louisville, but Smith told him to take Louisville on his own. With the Confederate army under Bragg prepared to take Louisville, the citizens of the town panicked. To make matters worse, General William "Bull" Nelson issued the following order: "The women and children of this city will prepare to leave the city without delay." He ordered the Jeffersonville ferry to be used for military purposes only. Private vehicles were not allowed to go aboard the ferry boats without a special permit. Hundreds of Louisville residents gathered at the wharf to be transported to New Albany or Jeffersonville. With Frankfort in Confederate hands, the State legislature held their sessions in the Jefferson County Courthouse. Troops, volunteers, and impressed labor worked around the clock to build a ring of breastworks and entrenchments around the city. New Union regiments flowed in. General Nelson took charge of the defense of Louisville. He sent Union troops to build pontoon bridges at Jeffersonville and New Albany to speed up the arrival of reinforcements, supplies, and if needed, the evacuation of the city.

Instead of taking Louisville, Bragg left Bardstown to install a Confederate governor at Frankfort. On September 26, 1862, 500 Confederate cavalrymen rode into the area of Eighteenth and Oak and captured 50 Union soldiers. The following night, a heavy skirmish occurred just beyond Middletown on the Shelbyville Pike and on September 30, Confederate and Union pickets fought at Gilman's Point in St. Matthews and pushed the Confederates back through Middletown to Floyd's Fork.

The War Department ordered Union General William Nelson to command the newly formed Army of the Ohio. When Louisville prepared for the Confederate army under Bragg, Union General Jefferson C. Davis, who could not reach his command under General Don Carlos Buell, met with General Nelson to offer his services. General Nelson gave him the command of the city militia. General Davis opened an office and went to work in assisting in the organization of the city militia. On Wednesday, General Davis visited General Nelson in his room at the Galt House. General Davis asked General

Nelson whether the brigade he assigned Davis was ready for service and asked if he could obtain arms for them. General Nelson asked Davis how many men were in his brigade. Davis responded that he had 2,500 men. General Nelson angrily barked to Davis: "About twenty-five hundred! About twenty-five hundred! By God! You a regular officer and come here to me and report about the number of men in your command? God damn you, don't you know, Sir, you should furnish me the exact number?" Davis told Nelson that he did not expect to get the guns now and only wanted to learn if he could get them and where, and after learning the exact number of troops, he would draw the needed weapons. General Nelson flew into a rage and screamed at General Davis: "About twenty-five hundred! By God I suspend you from your command, and order you to report to General Wright; and I've a damned mind to put you under arrest. Leave my room, Sir!"

Davis told General Nelson that he would not leave the room until he gave him an order. General Nelson barked: "The hell you won't! By God I'll put you under arrest, and send you out of the city under a provost guard! Leave my room, Sir!"

General Davis left the room, and, in order to avoid arrest, crossed over the river to Jeffersonville, where he remained until the next day, when General Stephen Gano Burbridge joined him. General Burbridge had also been relieved of command by General Nelson under a trivial cause. General Davis came to Cincinnati with General Burbridge and reported to General Wright, who ordered General Davis to return to Louisville and report to General Buell and General Burbridge to remain in Cincinnati. General Davis returned to Louisville and reported to Buell.

When General Davis saw General Nelson in the main hall of the Galt House, fronting the office, he asked Governor of Indiana, Oliver Morton to witness the conversation between him and General Nelson. The Governor agreed and the two walked up to General Nelson. General Davis confronted General Nelson and told him that he took advantage of his authority. General Nelson, sneeringly and placing a hand to his ear, said: "Speak louder, I don't hear very well." Davis in a louder tone repeated his statement. Nelson indignantly told Davis that he did not take advantage of his authority. Nelson told Davis that he threatened to have him arrested and sent out of the state under provost guard. Nelson took his hand and struck Davis twice in the face and stated: "There, damn you, take that!"

Davis left the room, but before he left he told Nelson, "This is not the last of it; you will hear from me again."

General Nelson turned to Governor Morton and asked him if he had come to insult him too. Governor Morton stated that he did not come to insult Nelson but requested that he be present and listen to the conversation between Nelson and Davis. General Nelson violently told the by-standers, "Did you hear the damned rascal insult me?" and walked into the ladies parlor. In three minutes, Davis returned, with a pistol he had borrowed from Captain Gibson of Louisville and walked toward the door that Nelson had passed through. He saw Nelson walk out of the parlor into the hall separating the main hall from the parlor, and the two faced each other ten yards apart. When General Davis drew his pistol and fired, the ball entered Nelson's heart. General Nelson threw up both hands and grabbed a gentlemen, who stood nearby, around the neck and exclaimed, "I am shot!" Nelson walked up the flight of stairs toward General Buell's room, but sank at the top of the stairs. Fellow officers took him to his room and they laid him on his bed. Nelson requested Reverend Mr. Talbott to see him at once. Mr. Talbott administered the ordinance of baptism. The General whispered, "It's all over," and died 15 minutes later.[192]

After the murder of General William Nelson, Union authorities placed General Davis under house arrest, but on October 13, 1862, Union authorities released him, because the period of his arrest without charge expired. Another reason for Davis' release may have been the shortage of generals in the field, and Buell needed every general in the field to take on Bragg's army.

Davis hired James Speed as his defense attorney. Governor Morton of Indiana and James Speed managed to delay General Davis's manslaughter indictment for two years and on May 24, 1864, the courts struck the criminal case against Davis from the docket. According to historian Jennifer Cole, James Speed took Davis's case, because Governor Oliver Morton or Lincoln pressured him to take the case, or he may have seen the case as a routine defense case that could increase his income, but the best explanation for why Speed

192 "The Murder of General Nelson," *Harper's Weekly*, October 18, 1862.

took Davis's case may have been the justification based on the principle of honor. Nelson had assaulted Davis's honor. Historian Bertram Wyatt-Brown wrote two major books on Southern honor, but honor also applied to Northern men to some extent. After being slapped in the face by Nelson, Davis had to avenge his honor. As Jennifer Cole pointed out murder or manslaughter may have been wrong, but an insult on one's honor was also wrong. Speed was a man of honor and may have believed that Davis was justified in his actions.[193] Union authorities involved in Davis's case may have thought that Davis was justified in his actions and let the case drop from the records, especially since Union General Jefferson Davis became a distinguished Union general during the Civil War.

With General Nelson dead, the command switched over to General Don Carlos Buell. On October 1, 1862, the Union army marched out of Louisville with 60,000 men. Buell sent a small Federal force to Frankfort to deceive Bragg as to the exact direction and location of the Federal army. The ruse worked. On October 4, 1862, the small Federal force attacked Frankfort, and Bragg left the city and headed back for Bardstown, thinking the entire Federal force was headed for Frankfort. Bragg decided that all Confederate forces should concentrate at Harrodsburg, Kentucky, ten miles northwest of Danville.

On October 6, 1862, Governor James Robinson met with Joshua Speed about an issue that would later have detrimental effects on how Kentucky viewed Lincoln and the military: the issue was over military and civilian courts. Joshua traveled to Washington, D.C., and met with his friend Lincoln and handed him a letter from Governor Robinson to Lincoln. In the letter, Robinson wrote that the Union army had marched out to meet Bragg's forces and hoped that the Union army overthrew the rebels and traitors in Kentucky, but the true purpose of his letter was to determine the "true line of demarcation between the civil and military authorities of the State." To secure and insure that the proper jurisdiction of the civil and military authorities should be ascertained, the civil authorities should be fixed by the Constitution and the laws of the United States and the State of Kentucky. The military authorities should be more indefinite, more dependent upon the circumstances under which the military is exercised and often to be declared by their Chief Executive

193 Jennifer Cole, "Semper Eadem: An Interpretation of the Life and Career of James Speed," 38-39.

Officers. All offenders taken into custody within military lines should be dealt with and punished by military authorities, all others by civil authorities. Robinson pointed out to Lincoln that all of Kentucky's judges, and jurors, were loyal men. Robinson sent copies of his letter to Generals Horatio Wright and Buell. He also approved of Provost Marshals if the offices were filled with proper men and if the marshals were given proper instructions as to their jurisdiction and the exercise of their powers.[194]

On October 8, 1862, Buell and Bragg fought at Perryville, Kentucky. Bragg's 16,000 men attacked Buell's 60,000 men. Federal forces suffered 845 dead, 2,851 wounded and 515 missing, while the Confederate toll was 3,396. Although Bragg won the Battle of Perryville tactically, he wisely decided to pull out of Perryville and link up with Smith. Once Smith and Bragg joined forces, Bragg decided to leave Kentucky and head for Tennessee.

On October 24, 1862, Lincoln replaced Union General Don Carlos Buell with Union General William Rosecrans. Most of the Union Army of the Ohio disliked Buell and rejoiced at his dismissal. James Speed wrote that Buell "failed to receive the confidence of his soldiers. He has inspired them with no enthusiasm. I do not believe that under his command they will accomplish anything. The want of trust in him will make many sick and many die who would otherwise get well."[195]

By mid-December James Speed became embroiled in a feud between two generals. Joshua informed his brother James that an effort arose to "poison" President Lincoln's mind against Union General Charles C. Gilbert of the 10th Division, Army of the Ohio. James Speed wrote to Lincoln that his son, John, a second lieutenant in the 9th Kentucky Cavalry, reported to General Gilbert that Colonel Thomas Snell of the 107th Illinois Infantry regiment lacked discipline. General Gilbert admired John Speed and recommended him to serve as a captain in the Adjutant General's Department. General Gilbert sent his Inspector to inspect Snell's command, who promptly brought charges against General Gilbert. Gilbert arrested Colonel Snell and threw him into a military prison. Snell escaped a military trial because he

194 James Robinson to Abraham Lincoln, Oct. 6, 1862, The Abraham Lincoln Papers, The Library of Congress, Washington, D.C.

195 Joseph Holt to Abraham Lincoln, October 28, 1862, The Abraham Lincoln Papers, The Library of Congress, Washington, D.C.

was never sworn into the United States military. Snell swore that he would "unhorse Gilbert." James Speed wrote to Lincoln that in his opinion Snell was never qualified for the office of colonel. The regiment lacked the proper authority and became so demoralized as to become a terror to the neighborhood and a disgrace to the army. Speed stated that the army needed discipline and officers who could enforce discipline. Kentucky suffered from marauding soldiers and need Gilbert's discipline.[196] Unfortunately, the government charged General Gilbert with mishandling his men at the Battle of Perryville in October 8, 1862, and relieved him from field command. For the rest of the war, he assumed a desk position as a major in the 19th U.S. Infantry.

As 1862 came to a close, the Union military managed to keep a major Confederate army out of the state. Although Joshua and James Speed disagreed with Lincoln's Emancipation Proclamation, Lincoln decided to issue a preliminary proclamation on September 22, 1862. The actual proclamation would not go into effect until January 1, 1863. Both Joshua and James Speed correctly assessed Kentucky's reaction to the proclamation, but Lincoln made sure the proclamation went into effect and went against his friends' advice. Although Joshua and James Speed disagreed with Lincoln on his emancipation proclamation, they held steadfast in their devotion to Lincoln and the Union.

---

196 James Speed to Abraham Lincoln, Dec. 17, 1862, The Abraham Lincoln Papers, The Library of Congress, Washington, D.C.

Chapter Nine

The Emancipation Proclamation

On January 1, 1863, Lincoln issued his official Emancipation Proclamation against the advice of Joshua and James. James thought the issue of emancipation was a state issue, not a federal issue. Joshua continued to believe that slavery was a state right. Both James and Joshua knew the backlash that befell anyone who supported the proclamation in Kentucky, but both brothers continued their support of the President.

On July 14, 1862, Lincoln convened a special invitation to the representatives and senators from the border states at the Executive Mansion. He urged an appeal to all the border states to compensated emancipation and asked for opinions. Charles Wickliffe, Garrett Davis, and John Crittenden from Kentucky responded that emancipation interfered with states rights and the appropriation involved was unconstitutional, the financial burden too great, and there were no funds to carry the plan into effect. Senator James Speed brought the sentiment expressed by the minority opinion to the Kentucky Senate. Speed was the only member who supported the measure. Kentucky rejected Lincoln's compensated emancipation plan.

In Lincoln's annual message to Congress, he proposed his plan of compensated emancipation to Congress. The plan stated that if a slave holding state abolished slavery before 1900, a specified sum of United States bonds would be paid to every slave to have been in the state by the census of 1860 and that any state who re-established slavery after receiving the compensation would refund the money to the government. The government also provided that all slaves freed by war would remain free and the property of loyal citizens should be paid for by the U.S. government at the same rate as provided in case of states abolishing slavery. Congress would also appropriate money or otherwise provide for voluntary colonizing of free blacks outside the United States, but Congress adjourned without bringing the matter to a vote.[197]

Abraham Lincoln's Emancipation Proclamation declared that all slaves in rebellious sections were free. Lincoln knew he did the right thing by issuing the Proclamation, ignoring the advice of not only the border-states, but also the advice of his friends. Ramifications arose from Kentucky's governor and the Kentucky General Assembly. Kentucky Governor James Robinson denounced the proclamation as a gross injustice in his message to the Kentucky legislature. He called upon the legislature to protest the Emancipation. The legislature became hostile toward Lincoln and talk arose in the state to recall all Kentucky Union troops, and there was some minimal advocacy of secession. The General Assembly met in Frankfort and voted that Lincoln's emancipation was "unwise, unconstitutional, and void." James Speed voted to agree with the statement. Rumors of secession flew across the state.[198]

On January 19, 1863, James wrote to his brother Joshua that he had returned from his home where he attended the criminal court. Since arriving back in Frankfort, he saw a few members of the Senate and wrote that the "negrophobia is nothing like as bad as it was at first. The rabid members are coming to their senses. Time is working wonders. If I am not mistaken, a vote of censure upon the Governor's message would pass the Senate. Its merits will be discussed. So far I am in no fear for Kentucky." He hoped that the present legislature would remain true and loyal to the Union.[199] Joshua forwarded the letter on to the President, who endorsed the letter.

On February 28, 1863, the Kentucky General Assembly debated the emancipation proclamation and adopted a set of 13 resolutions. The Fourth resolution stated that the Assembly protested the Emancipation Proclamation and declared the proclamation unconstitutional and void. James voted with the majority in favor of the resolution. The Sixth Resolution stated that the Assembly declined to accept the President's proposition for compensated emancipation, as contained in his proclamation of May 19, 1862. James voted against the

197 Helen Springer, "The Political Career of James Speed," (M.A. Thesis, University of Chicago, 1936), 65; E. Merton Coulter, *The Civil War and Readjustment in Kentucky*, (Chapel Hill: University of North Carolina Press, 1921, reprint Glouster, Mass, 1966), 158.

198 Helen Springer, 66; Coulter, 162.

199 James Speed to Joshua Speed, Jan. 19, 1863, The Abraham Lincoln Papers, The Library of Congress, Washington, D.C.

resolution.[200] James Speed agreed that the Emancipation Proclamation was unwise and unconstitutional, but he agreed with Lincoln's earlier proposal of compensated emancipation. James Speed thought that emancipation should be a state issue, not a federal issue.[201]

After Lincoln issued the Emancipation Proclamation, thousands of slaves and former slaves flocked to Union recruiting stations. Lincoln and Secretary of War Edwin Stanton established Camp Nelson, in Jessamine, Kentucky, as a black Union soldier recruiting station. The Kentucky legislature passed a resolution stating that raising black troops to defend the country and their supporters "have published to the world the atrocious libel upon the white man, that in his cowardice he appeals to the negro for protection." James voted against the resolution. The Senate reconsidered the resolution and changed the wording to state that the proposition to raise black soldiers to aid in putting down "this wicked rebellion, is an imputation upon the ability of the loyal whites to suppress it, and tends to weaken rather than strengthen the cause of the Union."[202] James voted with the majority of the Senate in favor of the resolution.

With Kentucky resenting the Emancipation Proclamation, the States Rights Party in Kentucky changed their name to the Democratic Party and gained advocates against the Unionist Party. On February 16, 1863, the Democratic Party called for a state convention to nominate a governor, six months before the election. Many feared that the Democratic Party would try to take the state out of the Union. The next day the House of Representatives voted 40-36 not to allow the Democratic Party to hold their convention.

On February 17, Colonel E.A. Gilbert called on his troops in Frankfort to fix bayonets and broke up the 200 Union Democratic Party delegates from 40 counties who met at the Metropolitan Hall. He called them traitors. Q. A. Gillmore, Union commander of central Kentucky, supported Colonel Gilbert's actions and stated that the members of the Democratic Party should be arrested as rebels.

On March 18-19, 1863, the Union Democratic Party held their convention in Louisville. General Jeremiah Boyle ran as a gubernatorial candidate. The party nominated Joshua Bell as governor and

200 Springer, 66-67.

201 Gary Lee Williams, "James and Joshua Speed: Lincoln's Kentucky Friends," (Ph.D. Dissertation, Duke University, 1971), 131-132.

202 Springer, 68-69.

Joshua Speed was a close friend and advisor to Abraham Lincoln for almost 30 years, dating from their first meeting in 1837 in Springfield, Illinois, through Lincoln's death in 1865.

James Speed, like his brother Joshua, was a trusted friend and advisor to President Lincoln, who turned to James to become attorney general shortly after the 1864 presidential election.

The family of John and Lucy Gilmer Fry Speed pose for artist J.S. Morton in 1864. Seated left to right are Susan Fry Speed Davis, Joshua Fry Speed, Lucy Gilmer Fry Speed (mother), William Pope Speed (who died in 1863), and Peachy Walker Speed Peay. Standing from left are Philip Speed, Lucy Fry Speed Breckinridge, James Speed, Martha Bell Speed Adams, and John Smith Speed. A portrait of family patriach John Speed, who died in 1841, is pictured above the family. (Portrait courtesy of Farmington Historic Home, Louisville, Ky.)

This gold watch is engraved "J. Speed 1811 on the reverse. Family history indicates that it was used by the U.S. Attorney General, James Speed, though it may have been passed down to him from his father. (Courtesy of Farmington Historic Home, Louisville, Ky.).

Above: Farmington, home of Joshua and Fanny Speed, is located in Louisville, Kentucky. The house and grounds have been restored to the original look of the period, and it is open to the public. Below: A plaque on the grounds of Farmington remembers the African-Americans who were enslaved at the plantation during the days of slavery.

Above: The summer kitchen/cook's quarters at Farmington This is a recent restoration based on the original foundation as well as an existing kitchen at a similar home built during the same time period. Below: The spring house at Farmington.

Top: A restored barn on the grounds of Farmington. Above: Using the original brick carriage house, along with an attached wood-frame barn, the last private owners of Farmington built the house above.

JANE,
WIFE OF
JAMES SPEED,
DIED MAY 3, 1886,
AGED 72 YEARS.

Opposite page: The grave marker for James Speed and his wife Jane. This page: The grave marker for Joshua and Fanny Speed. Both couples are buried in Cave Hill Cemetery in Louisville, Kentucky.

Several notable figures of nineteenth-century Kentucky are buried in Cave Hill Cemetery in Louisville, Kentucky, including (clockwise from above) James Guthrie, president of the Louisville and Nashville Railroad, as well as a president of the University of Louisville and Secretary of the Treasury under President Franklin Pierce; Lovell Rousseau, a Kentucky state senator commissioned by President Abraham Lincoln to organize Kentucky's home guard for protection against possible Confederate invasion; and Thomas Bramlette, governor of Kentucky during the Civil War.

LOVELL HARRISON ROUSSEAU
INDIANA LEGISLATURE 1844
ROUSSEAU

Aged 58 Years

This page: The Abraham Lincoln monument in Springfield, Illinois. Opposite page: The monument is surrounded by sculptures such as this one.

ABRAHAM LINCOLN
1809–1865

MARY TODD
LINCOLN
1818 — 1882

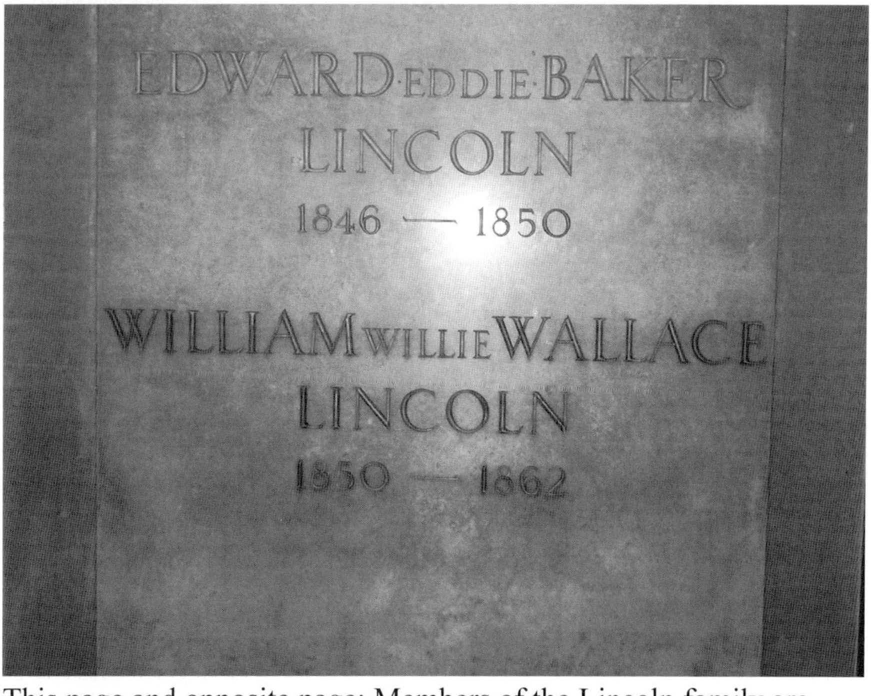

This page and opposite page: Members of the Lincoln family are interred at the Lincoln monument in Springfield, Illinois.

Statue of Abraham Lincoln in front of the Louisville (Kentucky) Public Library. This statue was sculpted by George Grey Barnard and was presented to the city of Louisville in 1922 by Mr. and Mrs. Isaac W. Bernheim.

Richard Jacob as lieutenant governor. Bell stepped down, because of the domination of the state by military authorities. On April 13, 1863, General Ambrose Burnside issued Order Number 38, which stated that all persons within Union lines who aided the Confederacy would be tried for treason. Even those people who merely declared their support for the Confederacy were subject to exile beyond Federal lines. On May 2, 1863, the Union Democratic Committee nominated Thomas Bramlette, a former commander in the Union army, as governor.[203] Many of the Unionists did not support Bramlette as the nominee for governor and broke off to form their own party called the Peace Democrats and nominated Charles Wickliffe as governor. During the campaign, the Union Democrats denied that they supported the Lincoln administration and the Emancipation Proclamation. The Kentucky Peace Democrats also claimed they did not support the Lincoln administration and hoped to end the reign of "despotism which crushes her [Kentucky] personal and political liberties."[204]

On July 10, Governor Robinson issued his proclamation that anyone who had been expatriated according to the war legislation were disenfranchised and could not vote. On July 31, 1864, General Ambrose Burnside declared martial law throughout the state and silenced civil authorities who tried to interfere. His reasoning was to prevent disloyal Kentuckians from voting. On July 25, General Jeremiah Boyle also issued an order that anyone voting for Charles Wickliffe of the Peace Democrats would be considered a rebel. Boyle issued an order stating any person who wanted to vote and was unable to establish the right should be arrested and held as a rebel. Each voter had to take an oath stating: "I do solemnly swear that I have never entered the service of the so-called Confederate States; that I have not been engaged in the service of the so-called 'provisional government of Kentucky,' either in a civil or military capacity; that I have never, either directly or indirectly, aided the rebellion, and am willing to furnish men and money for the vigorous prosecution of the war against the rebellious league known as the Confederate States; so help me God."[205] Wickliffe and the Peace Democrats lost the election and Bramlette won for the Union Democratic Party.

203 Coulter, 171-172.
204 Coulter, 174.
205 Ibid., 177.

With Burnside's Order Number 38, Joshua Speed became involved in the case of Mrs. Margaret Preston. Mrs. Preston's husband, William C. Preston, joined the Confederacy. The Union army sent Mrs. Preston and her family south. Joshua Speed wrote Lincoln a letter stating that although he agreed with the order, he thought that there should be an exception to the rule. Joshua wrote that Mrs. Preston behaved with "the utmost propriety and is not responsible for the actions of her husband. You know who she is, so long as she can remain within the reach of her property she has the means of living—she has been accustomed to all the luxuries of life—If she is sent across our lines where her friends here can not assist her—her condition would be almost destitute."[206] General Preston wrote a letter to his wife telling her not to act against the federal government and Joshua Speed felt that Mrs. Preston kept her husband's request. Joshua stated that Mrs. Preston was a woman of high social position and had great family influence, but did not use them against the government. He wrote to Lincoln that Mrs. Preston was a cripple, and her son could not be moved because of ill health. He pleaded on her behalf asking that the order to remove Mrs. Preston to be revoked and offer clemency to a "meritorious" person.

On September 19-20, 1863, Confederate General Braxton Bragg and Union General William Rosecrans fought a series of major battles at Chickamauga, Georgia. On September 20, a gap opened in the Union lines and Confederate forces poured through the gap, leading to Union General Rosecrans and half of his army to be swept from the field. The Union army fell back to Chattanooga, Tennessee. Union and Confederate casualties amounted to 2,312 Confederate dead, 14,674 wounded, and 1,469 missing or captured; Union losses amounted to 1,657 dead, 9,756 wounded, and 4,757 missing or captured. During the battle, Confederate forces overran Union General Thomas Crittenden's XXI Corps, which led Union General William Rosecrans to remove General Thomas Crittenden from command. Joshua Speed came to Crittenden's defense. He wrote to Lincoln that he desired a speedy investigation into General Crittenden's case. He stated that General Crittenden had distinguished himself at Shiloh and Stone's River and the Union army promoted Crittenden for his action at Shiloh. At the Battle of Stone's River he gained the

206 Joshua Speed to Abraham Lincoln, May 22, 1863, The Abraham Lincoln Papers, The Library of Congress, Washington, D.C.

plaudits of all who saw him. Crittenden told Joshua Speed that "if there is any two days of his life for which deserves more credit than that rendered to his country at the Battle of Chickamauga he would not know where to select them."[207] Joshua Speed wrote that Crittenden did not know he was writing to Lincoln. He also wrote that he liked Thomas Crittenden, but he liked Lincoln and the Union cause better. He stated that if an investigation found Crittenden guilty, "strike him from the roll–if he has acted well his part sustain him."[208] A court of inquiry acquitted Thomas Crittenden of all charges, but his career still carried the scar of the Union loss at Chickamauga. The Union command transferred Crittenden to the Army of the Potomac, where he led the 1st Division, IX Corps, until 1864. When he asked for his resignation from the army on June 9, 1864, the army agreed to his request and Crittenden left the army in December 1864.

As 1863 came to a close, Kentucky's political landscape changed when Lincoln issued his Emancipation Proclamation. The Peace Democrats and Union Democratic Party both stood against Lincoln. Joshua and James Speed did not agree with Lincoln's Emancipation Proclamation, but they both stood by Lincoln. Both brothers became disillusioned with the Union Democratic Party and looked for a new party who supported Lincoln. James Speed, along with Reverend Robert J. Breckinridge, formed the new Unconditional Unionists Party, which stood for the crushing of the rebellion, emancipation, and the support of black Union soldiers. James Speed became a radical in his state and supported federal emancipation. Joshua Speed also changed his view on slavery and supported the new Unconditional Party. Both brothers fought against the tide of Kentuckians who turned away from the Union and Lincoln.

207 Joshua Speed to Abraham Lincoln, November 6, 1863, The Abraham Lincoln Collection, The Library of Congress, Washington, D.C.

208 Ibid.

Chapter Ten

Joining the Unconditional Union Party

In early 1864, both Joshua and James Speed became disillusioned with the Union Democratic Party and looked for a new party who supported Lincoln. The Kentucky Union Democratic Party under Governor Thomas Bramlette did not agree with Lincoln's recruitment of black Union soldiers and his emancipation policy. James Speed, along with Reverend Robert J. Breckinridge, formed the new Unconditional Unionists Party, which stood for the crushing of the rebellion, emancipation, and the support of black Union soldiers. James Speed became a radical in his state and supported federal emancipation. Joshua Speed also changed his view on slavery and supported the new Unconditional Unionist Party. Both brothers fought against the tide of Kentuckians who turned away from the Lincoln administration.

On January 12, 1864, General Jeremiah Boyle resigned as Military Commander for the District of Kentucky. On February 14, 1864, Major General Ulysses Grant ordered Union Brigadier General Stephen Gano Burbridge to Camp Nelson, located in southern Jessamine County, Kentucky, to command the District of Kentucky until relieved by General Jacob Ammen, who was on court-martial duty. When he was relieved by General Ammen, Burbridge would report to Grant for an assignment. By Order Number 41, Burbridge was assigned to command the District of Kentucky.[209]

On that same day, January 12, 1864, James Speed became involved in the case of A.Z. Boyer, Company C, Second Kentucky Cavalry, C. S. A. Union authorities confined Boyer to a prison in Louisville, Kentucky, after he was convicted as a spy. Union authorities sentenced Boyer to death by hanging. Mr. C.W. Castleman went to

209 O.R. Series I, vol. XXXII/2 Union Correspondence, Orders, and Returns Relating to Operations in Kentucky, Southwest Va, Tennessee, Mississippi, Alabama, and North Georgia, from January 1, 1864 to February 29, 1864.

Washington to meet with President Lincoln for the purpose of asking Lincoln to pardon Boyer. James Speed and Robert Breckinridge recommended Castleman, who had proof of Boyer's innocence, which had not been presented at Boyer's trial. Several days later, on January 18, 1864, Lincoln asked that Boyer take the oath of December 8, 1863. After he took the oath he would be pardoned and discharged. On January 29, 1864, under Special Orders No. 45, Union authorities released Boyer from custody.[210]

On February 22, the Kentucky legislature, controlled by Union Democrats, passed a resolution that protested the enlistment of blacks for army service and added a request, directed at President Abraham Lincoln, to remove camps for United States black troops beyond the state lines. The legislature also prohibited any recruiting other than that of the United States and each recruit could be fined $500 and imprisoned from two to six months if the rule was violated. Union authorities ignored the Kentucky legislature and ordered Union General James B. Fry, United States Provost Marshall, to enroll all male blacks in Kentucky between 18 and 45.[211] Although the Kentucky legislature disagreed with the recruitment of black soldiers, James Speed felt that the Federal government had the right and power to enlist them. He believed that freed and enslaved blacks could and should be allowed to fight in the Union army and supported the United States Colored Troops.[212] He also felt that the federal government had the ability and the right to change the laws protecting slavery.[213]

Although James Speed belonged to the Union Democratic Party, he did not like the party's platform, which disliked Lincoln's military rule in Kentucky and emancipation. He also did not agree with the party's stance against the recruitment of black soldiers. The issue of black recruitment broke apart the Union Democratic Party. In February of 1864, James Speed worked on the "Border Slave State Emancipation Convention" in Louisville. The convention supported

---

210 Brutus Clay to Abraham Lincoln, January 14, 1864, The Abraham Lincoln Papers, The Library of Congress, Washington, D. C.; Roy Basler, ed., *Collected Works of Abraham Lincoln*, Vol. 7, (The Abraham Lincoln Association, 1953).

211 The Military Department of Kentucky, *Military History of Kentucky*, (The American Guide Series, Works Projects Administration, 1936), 205.

212 Jennifer Cole, "Semper Eadem: An Interpretation of the Life and Career of James Speed," (M.A. Thesis University of Louisville, 2003), 42.

213 Cole, 42-43.

the United States Colored Troops and a constitutional amendment to abolish slavery.[214]

On March 8, 1864, General Burbridge laid the groundwork on how to deal with guerrilla warfare and those he claimed were disloyal citizens. To show that he did not invent his orders against guerrillas, he published the Acts of the Kentucky Legislature. Burbridge used the acts in almost every one of his controversial orders during his military command in Kentucky. What Kentucky citizens failed to realize was that he only carried out Kentucky's acts passed by the legislature. Unfortunately, Burbridge carried out the Kentucky acts to the letter of the law with no restraint. He stated that all acts passed by the Kentucky Legislature concerning civil law would be relied on in military cases. In Act 548 of the Kentucky Legislature, the act stated that if any person should counsel, advise, aid, assist, encourage, or induce any officer or soldier of the Confederate States, or any guerilla, robber, bandit, or armed band, or persons or person engaged, or professing to be engaged in making or levying war upon the United States government or the State of Kentucky, or upon any Kentucky citizen or resident, to destroy or injure any property of Kentucky, or shall counsel, encourage, aid, advise, or assist any such person or persons to injure, arrest, kidnap, or otherwise maltreat any citizen or resident of Kentucky, or shall harbor or conceal or shall voluntarily receive or aid any such persons, would be guilty of a high misdemeanor, and upon conviction would be fined between $100 and $10,000, or confined in the county jail between six months and twelve months, and could be both fined and jailed at the discretion of the jury.[215]

The legislature also stated that if any person spoke or wrote against the U. S. government or of Kentucky, or favored the Confederate States and helped to excite the people of Kentucky to insurrection or rebellion against the authority or laws of Kentucky or of the United States, or who would willfully attempt to terrify or prevent by threats or otherwise the Kentucky citizens from supporting and maintaining the legal and constitutional authority of the Federal Government or of Kentucky, or endeavor to prevent or shall opposed

214 Ibid, 44.

215 O.R. Series I, Vol. XXXII/3 Union Correspondence, Orders, and Returns Relating to Operations in Kentucky, Southwest Va, Tennessee, Mississippi, Alabama, and North Georgia, from March 1, 1864 to April 30, 1864. Order No. 29.

the suppression of the existing rebellion against the authority of the Federal government, every such person would be legally convicted and be fined $100 to $5,000, or confined in the county jail between six months to a year, or both. The act stated that the constitutional right of speaking or writing in reference to the manner of administering the government, state or national, or against the conduct of any officer of either, when done in good faith with the intent of defending and preserving either of the said governments or of exposing and correcting the maladministration of either government or the misconduct of any officer, civil or military, would not be interred with.[216]

The act also stated that any person who did not give information to the nearest military authorities or civil officer of the presence in, or raid, or approach of any guerilla or guerillas in the vicinity would be guilty of a misdemeanor and if convicted would be fined between $100 to $1,000 or confined in a county jail between three months and six months, or both.[217]

In any trial, the jury would hear whether the character and reputation of the accused was loyal or disloyal to the government of the United States. The test of loyalty of the defendant or defendants would be whether they adhered to and supported the Constitution of the United States and Kentucky and complied with all their laws. Any Kentucky attorney who violated any of the provisions of the act would be debarred from practicing law.[218]

The act also stated that if any Confederate soldier or body of soldiers, or armed bands belonging to the Confederacy, or the Confederate Provisional government of Kentucky, or any armed band not acting under the authority of the U.S. or Kentucky, or any guerilla or guerillas, should injure or destroy or take or carry away any property of any person, county, city, corporate body, association, or congregation of Kentucky, or would arrest, kidnap, imprison, or wound would be entitled to recover damages as a jury may find and if dead, his wife or personal representative or heir of law, would be entitled to recover damages to the same extent that the person himself might for any of said injuries if death had not ensued and for the property injured, destroyed, taken or carried away, the person, city, corporation, body, association, or congregation so injured should be

216 Ibid.
217 Ibid.
218 Ibid.

entitled to recover double the value of damages and the damages of any of said injuries may be recovered of any persons doing any of said wrongful acts, and of any person or persons who shall aid, advise, abet, encourage or counsel such acts, would harbor conceal, aid, or encourage such wrongdoing or would permit, when it was in his power to prevent it, any member of his family living with him under his control so to aid, abet, advise, encourage, or counsel such acts, or harbor, conceal, aid or encourage such wrongdoers may be sued jointly with or without such wrongdoers, or some or any or all may be sued until the damages sustained as above provided may have been recovered by the party or parties aggrieved. Any disloyal person who had knowledge of the presence within the county of his residence of such guerilla or guerillas or predatory band, and failed to give immediate notice to either civil or military authorities would be guilty of aiding, harboring, and abetting the wrongdoer and be held jointly and severally reliable with such wrongdoers for all illegal acts done by such guerillas or predatory band.[219]

On March 14, 1863, Union General Ulysses S. Grant wrote to Union Major General John Schofield that General Burbridge "seems to be doing so well in Kentucky that I think he had better be retained permanently in the command of the district."[220] On that same day, Governor Bramlette wrote to Burbridge that he was not able to meet with Burbridge in his headquarters at Louisville because he had an appointment with Doctor Robert Breckinridge. He was going to send Doctor Breckinridge on a mission to Washington, D.C. to save them from a collision over the question of recruiting slaves into the Union army. Bramlette was determined to carry out his laws, and if any man violated them he must abide the penalty. Bramlette stated that the forcible abduction of slaves, the enlistment without consent of owners, enticing them to run away, were against the known laws of Kentucky. Bramlette stated that the duty of every Union officer was to arrest the violators and hand them over to the Civil Magistrates for trial. He wrote that if the President assumes that he had a right to command these violations, Kentucky's laws deny it. If the President would submit to the judicial determination of the question as to whether to recruit black soldiers, if not it will become Bramlette's duty was to uphold and maintain his laws which have been

219 Ibid.
220 Ibid.

constitutionally enacted by all the powers with which he was enacted. To maintain and enforce the law against those accused of its violation was his duty, and he would uphold them to the utmost of his ability. But he wrote to Burbridge that he wished to avoid if possible any semblance of collision with the President and therefore would use every means to resolve the problem.[221]

On March 16, 1864, Burbridge sent a telegram to President Lincoln stating that he had spent the night with Governor Bramlette and heard his proclamation concerning the recruitment of black soldiers. He reported that the speech had a national ring to it and stated Kentucky would do her duty to the Nation. He wrote that there was no need for fear about the enrollment of black soldiers in Kentucky, that the law would be obeyed.[222]

On March 23, Governor Bramlette met with Dr. Robert Breckinridge, accompanied by Archibald Dixon and A.G. Hodges. Dixon and Hodges met with President Lincoln. The conference ended with a compromise where the Governor assented to black enrollment on the condition that no enlistment of blacks would take place so long as Kentucky continued to furnish their quota of white men.[223]

On April 4, Colonel Frank Wolford and Lieutenant Governor Richard T. Jacob spoke at Paris, Kentucky. Immense crowds gathered during court day in Bourbon County. Men came to town to horse trade and buy cattle. Auctions were held for land and slaves. On the April court day in central Kentucky, counties held their horse shows, and in the square around the court house, livestock and thoroughbreds went up for auction. With a massive audience already present, Colonel Wolford and Lieutenant Governor Jacob gave their speeches. Both men spoke out against black recruitment.[224]

Burbridge issued an order on April 8, 1864, stating that the Acting Assistant Provost Marshal General was authorized to receive recruits into the United States service black males offered by their owners. The camp of instruction was to be established in Kentucky, but the black recruits as soon as they were enlisted and mustered into

221 Letter from Governor Bramette to General Stephen G. Burbridge, March 14, 1864, Frankfort, Kentucky. Stephen Gano Burbridge letters, 1 reel of microfilm, University of Kentucky Special Collections and Digital Programs, Lexington, Kentucky.

222 O.R. Series III, Vol. IV, [#125] March 16, 1864, Dispatch from Burbridge to Lincoln.

223 *Military History of Kentucky*, 207.

224 Loraine Butler, *John Morgan and His Men* (Philadelphia: Dorrance & Company, 1960), 293.

service, were to be sent to Gallatin, Nashville, and Clarksville, Tennessee.[225] Governor Bramlette appointed J.P. Flint commissioner and agent to visit black Union camps and obtain for their legal owners proper vouchers. Bramlette also appointed Flint to obtain evidence for enlistments of Kentucky black troops in Tennessee and other states to allow Kentucky to obtain proper credits against the state's quota for troops.[226]

With Burbridge supporting the recruitment of Union black soldiers, many Union Democrats and members of the Kentucky legislature worked against Burbridge and asked for his removal. On May 6, 1864, James Speed, Blank Ballard, T.S. Bell, W.D. Gallagher, and Joshua Tevis wrote to Lincoln in support of Burbridge's recruitment of black Union soldiers. James Speed and the other members of the letter felt that Burbridge's removal would be a "calamity." They also stated that Burbridge was a "true and faithful lover of his country. He is wholly for his Country, not for himself. We are intimately acquainted with his proceedings in the District of Kentucky. They command the confidence of every loyal man who understands his Conduct."[227] Governor Bramlette supported General Burbridge. Burbridge and Governor Bramlette became friends from when both had commanded Union regiments. Governor Bramlette was one of the petitioners to have Burbridge command in Kentucky.

In May of 1864, Robert J. Breckinridge formed the Unconditional Union Party, which stood for the crushing of the rebellion and the liberation of the slaves. The party supported the re-election of President Lincoln. James Speed served on the party's central committee, committee on organization, and committee on resolutions at the state convention on May 25, 1864. Speed abandoned his Union Democratic Party and aligned himself with the radicals in the state. James and Joshua attended the Unconditional Unionists convention. During the May 25, 1864, convention, the Unconditional Union Committee appointed James a delegate to the (Union) Republican National Convention in Baltimore, along with Robert Breckinridge, and several other members of the Unconditional Unionists Party. Joshua

---

225 Richard Sears, *Camp Nelson, Kentucky: A Civil War History*, (Lexington: The University Press of Kentucky, 2002), 54.

226 *Military History of Kentucky*, 208.

227 Bland Ballard et. al. to Abraham Lincoln, May 6, 1864, The Abraham Lincoln Papers, The Library of Congress, Washington, D.C.

helped the new party by establishing a pro-Lincoln paper called the *Constitutional Union Press*, later called the *Union Press*.

The Union Democratic Party, led by George Prentice and James Guthrie, held their convention. The Peace Democrats, led by Charles Wickliffe, Senator Lazarus Powell, and J. H. Harney held their convention on June 28, 1864.[228]

On June 25, General Henry Halleck ordered General Burbridge to declare martial law in Kentucky. He was to arrest all disloyal citizens in Kentucky who gave aid and assistance to armed rebels and sought to incite insurrection and rebellion. He also stated that among the aiders and abettors of rebellion and treason were distinguished officers of state government and members of Congress. Secretary of War Stanton directed Burbridge, under the authority of the President, to arrest and send all persons inciting insurrection or aiding and abetting the enemy to Washington. The President gave Burbridge authority to use the military, and if necessary to call upon Major General Samuel Heintzelman and the commanding officer in Tennessee for assistance. Halleck instructed Burbridge to use discretion, but at the same time promptly and energetically arrest the people guilty of insurrection and aiding or abetting the enemy. He wrote to Burbridge that any attempt at rebellion in Kentucky "must be put down with a strong hand, and traitors must be punished without regard to their rank or sex."

On July 5, Lincoln renewed the suspension of the writ of habeas corpus in Kentucky and declared martial law. Burbridge wrote to Stanton that he would spare no effort to protect loyal citizens and carry into effect the enlistment of troops, black or white, and suppress treasonable and disloyal practices within his command.

On July 7, 1864, Abraham Lincoln paroled Colonel Frank Wolford and allowed him to proceed to Louisville, Kentucky, and remain until his trial in court. Frank Wolford promised not to speak in public. However, Union authorities imprisoned Frank Wolford in Knoxville, Tennessee, for making a speech against using blacks as soldiers, for which he was tried for disloyalty and dismissed from the service.[229] On July 10, 1864, Colonel Frank Wolford returned to Louisville from

228 Helen Springer, "The Political Career of James Speed," (M.A. Thesis, University of Chicago, Illinois, 1936), 70-71.

229 Abraham Lincoln, Parole for Frank Wolford, July 7, 1864, The Abraham Lincoln Papers, The Library of Congress, Washington, D.C.

Washington, D.C., under parole. Thirteen charges pended against him as a result of his campaign speeches. The Federal government allowed Wolford to return to Kentucky to stand trial on the various charges before a military court. The next day, Governor Bramlette wrote to Colonel Richard T. Jacob in reference to Colonel Wolford's arrest, stating that the "loyal people of Kentucky cannot be provoked or driven into rebellion against the government, but in self defense might justly retaliate political arrests–upon those who, among our own citizens, urge or provoke political arrests, and seek to inaugurate political terrorism. By this time, Dr. Robert Breckinridge no longer held esteem with Governor Bramlette, because Breckinridge protested against the raising of troops in Kentucky for home defense and placing them under the command of Governor Bramlette and Colonel Wolford. Colonel Wolford was a Union Democrat who supported Union General George B. McClellan as President. Breckinridge was an Unconditional Union Party man who nominated the re-election of Lincoln for President.[230] On July 17, Lincoln sent James Speed another parole for Wolford to sign.

On July 30, 1864, Burbridge acted on information he had gathered about a secret conspiracy in Kentucky. He ordered the arrest of the leading members in Louisville, Kentucky, who belonged to the Sons of Liberty. Burbridge also ordered the arrest of Kentucky Judge Joshua Bullitt, Chief Justice of Kentucky. As the ferry between Jeffersonville, Indiana, and Louisville, Kentucky, prepared to leave the wharf, Federal agents arrested Bullitt. During the next two weeks, military authorities arrested Dr. Henry F. Kalfus, W.K. Thomas, Alfred Harris, G.S.G. Payne, Joseph R. Buchanan, Thomas Jeffries, J.J. Paul, John Hines, John Colgan, Henry Stickrod, Michael Carroll, William Fitzhenry, Erwin Bell, A.J. Brannon, Thomas Miller, A.J. Mitchell, John Rudd, Charles J. Clarke, B.C. Redford, John H. Talbott and W.G. Gray, who were residents of Jefferson County and Louisville, Kentucky. On July 28, 1864, Union spy Felix Stidger learned in Indianapolis that a day had been set for an armed uprising by the Sons of Liberty. Alarmed by the news, Stidger met with Union General Henry Carrington, Governor Oliver Morton of Indiana, Governor Bramlette, Burbridge, and Colonel T.B. Fairleigh. Stidger told the assembly that 1,500 trained and well armed men were ready to attack Camp Morton at Indianapolis and free 6,000 Confederate prisoners.

230 *Military History of Kentucky*, 207.

Nearby, he also reminded them that the state and Federal arsenals had enough arms to equip 6,000 men. In Kentucky, Stidger told the council that a band of members were waiting for the signal to set the whole city of Louisville afire with Greek fire. Seven regiments of seasoned Confederate soldiers were hiding their arms, waiting to assemble on the day of the uprising.[231]

Three weeks later, Elizabeth Bullitt, Joshua Bullitt's wife, and Joshua Speed wrote to Lincoln about Joshua Bullitt's secret arrest. General Burbridge did not allow Joshua Bullitt to inform his family of his arrest and kept him prisoner at Barracks Number One in Louisville for two weeks. Elizabeth Bullitt asked to visit her husband, but Burbridge denied the request. Elizabeth Bullitt demanded of Burbridge that Joshua Bullitt should have a trial before the Kentucky Civil Courts, but Burbridge did not even take notice of the request. During Joshua Bullitt's imprisonment a military investigation of the charges was made, but he was never informed of the charges. Military authorities did not ask Bullitt a single question in regard to the charges against him, nor was anyone allowed to give evidence on his behalf. Military authorities kept the testimony against Bullitt secret. Elizabeth Bullitt felt that the charges against Bullitt consisted solely of papers and letters said to have been found in his carpet bag and in the hands of certain military parties. Elizabeth Bullitt wrote to Lincoln that had Bullitt been given a fair civilian trial, he believed that documents taken from his carpet bag were planted and that certain letters were forgeries. Joshua Bullitt assured his wife Elizabeth that he had no papers in his possession of a treasonable character, nor had he ever written letters attributed to him, and Elizabeth Bullitt testified that Joshua Bullitt's "word is truth."[232]

After two weeks of imprisonment, Burbridge sent Joshua Bullitt and others to Memphis, and General Burbridge told Elizabeth Bullitt that Bullitt might visit his sick family and make some necessary business arrangements and that "it was not yet determined whether he would be sent off to the Dry Tortugas or to South America."[233] Elizabeth Bullitt appealed to Lincoln that he would not allow the ruthless proceedings against Joshua Bullitt and that if the sentence of

231 Robert McDowell, *City of Conflict: Louisville in the Civil War 1861-1865*, (Louisville Civil War Roundtable Publishers, 1962), 166-167.

232 Elizabeth Bullitt and Joshua Speed to Abraham Lincoln, August 26, 1864, The Abraham Lincoln Collection, The Library of Congress, Washington, D.C.

233 Ibid.

banishment was to be enforced, that Joshua Bullitt be sent to Canada, where his family could join him and where his health would not suffer in a hotter climate.[234] Elizabeth Bullitt also asked Lincoln that before Burbridge sent Joshua Bullitt away that he be allowed to come home for a period of time in order to make arrangements for the welfare of his family and the payment of his debts. He also asked Lincoln to deliver to him $1,068.25 in gold coins, taken from Bullitt's carpet bag at the time of his arrest and paid over to General Ewing to the Quartermasters Department, whose receipt Elizabeth Bullitt had in his possession. The money belonged to Joshua Bullitt, but military authorities refused to give Elizabeth Bullitt the money on grounds that the money belonged to a secret organization. Elizabeth Bullitt demanded the money and again military authorities refused to give him the money, since Joshua Bullitt was a conspirator and had "no right to the money even if it was his." Elizabeth Bullitt wrote to Lincoln that the charges were made, but not proven, and asked Lincoln to order the money paid to him.

Joshua Speed wrote to Lincoln that Elizabeth Bullitt showed him the letter, which he forwarded on to him. He stated that the appeal of Bullitt's wife is "natural and touching, and I know will touch your own good heart; whatever your duty may require you to do in the premises." Joshua Speed vaguely knew about the charges against Joshua Bullitt. Joshua Bullitt was Joshua Speed's kinsman, since their mothers were sisters. Joshua did not know upon what terms Bullitt would accept his liberty or exile to any country, but he did know that if the terms were offered, and he accepted, he would hold to his promise. Joshua Speed asked General Ewing about the money. Ewing confirmed that the money was gold, and that he was certain that the money belonged to Judge Bullitt and to no one else. He said that under the law, he had paid the money over to the Quartermaster Department and handed a copy of General Allen's receipt with a request that Joshua Speed would hand the receipt over to Mrs. Bullitt. Joshua Speed hoped that Lincoln would pay the money to Elizabeth Bullitt. Joshua Bullitt needed the money for the support of his family and the payment of his debts. Union authorities did not release Bullitt until November of 1864, but Bullitt feared that Burbridge might arrest him again, so he fled to Canada for safety.[235]

234 Ibid.
235 Ibid.

On October 26, Jane Speed, James's wife, asked Lincoln to transfer her son, Captain John Speed, Assistant Adjutant General, to another department. Captain John Speed served in the 9th Kentucky Cavalry as a captain in the Adjutant General's Department under General Charles Gilbert's command, but served with General William T. Sherman throughout the Atlanta Campaign. When the city of Atlanta fell to Sherman's forces on September 2, 1864, Captain John Speed came home on furlough. Jane Speed noticed when John arrived home, he was broken in health. He still wished to serve his country until the rebellion came to an end, but felt he must serve his time in a les arduous field. The Pay Department was suggested and a position John Speed was particularly fitted for. She wrote to Lincoln that neither James nor John knew about her "possession with the idea that perhaps an application on any part might be successful."[236] She hoped that Lincoln would grant her case, but asked that he did not let John Speed know about her application.

On November 8, 1864, President Lincoln was re-elected President of the United States. Democratic candidate Union General George B. McClellan received 61,486 votes in Kentucky, while Lincoln only received 26,592. Lincoln received majorities in 25 counties out of the 101 reporting and in 56 counties he received over 100 votes. In only eight counties did McClellan receive over 100 votes. Historian E. Merton Coulter stated that there were 54,000 fewer votes cast in the 1864 election than in 1860, which indicated the great demoralization which prevailed over the state. He wrote that "although military interference was not nearly so glaring as it had been in previous elections, still some of the falling off must be attributed to intimidation by the army, for [Robert] Breckinridge and [General Stephen] Burbridge sedulously worked to create the impression that the test of loyalty, which meant payment for slaves and property seized and freedom from arrest and persecution, would be determined by the way a person voted-if he voted at all. And many, doubtless, considered no record better than a bad one–hence they stayed at home."[237]

In November of 1864, General Burbridge ordered the arrest of Lieutenant Governor Richard T. Jacob. Jacob served as commander

236 Jane Speed to Abraham Lincoln, Series 1, General Correspondence, October 26, 1864, The Abraham Lincoln Papers, The Library of Congress, Washington, D.C.

237 E. Merton Coulter, *The Civil War and Readjustment in Kentucky*, (Chapel Hill: The University of North Carolina Press, 1921, reprint, Glouster, Mass, 1966), 187-188.

of the 9th Kentucky Cavalry, the same unit James Speed's son, John Speed, served as a Captain. Jacob was a Kentucky Union Democratic Party member, who resigned his position in the 9th Kentucky and in 1863, was elected Lieutenant Governor. He spoke out against Lincoln's Emancipation Proclamation and became an opponent to Lincoln's administration. Jacob refused to enlist black soldiers and campaigned for George B. McClellan in 1864. With the arrests of Colonel Frank Wolford, Judge Joshua Bullitt and Lieutenant Governor Jacob by General Burbridge, 47 purported Kentucky Unionists, including Joshua Speed, sent Governor Bramlette a letter petitioning him to release Jacob. Bramlette wrote to Lincoln stating that both Wolford and Jacob were "incorruptible patriots and invincibly devoted to the preservation of the Union and for the suppression of rebellion." Governor Bramlette stated that the affidavits against Jacob and Wolford were made "in some dark corner—extra judicial and exparte—by men who are afraid to avow their infamy in the face of an open tribunal, face to face with the men they accuse—constitute the foundation of their arrest." He also stated that the false acquisitions came from a "secret inquisition" to condemn men without a trial and punish without a hearing. He wrote that Jacob and Wolford were veteran soldiers and not rebel sympathizers and that the rebels are rejoicing to hear that "the brave and gallant Jacob, the indomitable Wolford, the hero of more conflicts than any man who has battles against rebellion—have turned to the side of rebellion!!!! How it must revive their hopes and cheer them on to keep up the struggle a little longer! For if Jacob and Wolford have turned Rebels, surely all Kentucky will soon come shouting to the Rebel banner."[238] He asked that Lincoln either release or suspend the order for Jacob's and Wolford's banishment to the south. Governor Bramlette had an ongoing feud with Union General Stephen Burbridge and his biggest supporters, the Unconditional Unionists, led by Rev. Robert Breckinridge. Lincoln telegraphed Governor Bramlette that he had received his letter. Lincoln, General Samuel Suddarth, commander of the Kentucky State Militia, Albert Hodges, and the Secretary of War Edwin Stanton met to try and devise a means of pacification and harmony for

238 Thomas Bramlette to Abraham Lincoln, Nov. 22, 1864, The Abraham Lincoln Papers, The Library of Congress, Washington, D.C.

Kentucky.[239] The only way Lincoln could affect any peace in Kentucky was to relieve General Burbridge of command. In February 1865, Secretary of War Edwin Stanton relieved General Burbridge of command and replaced him with General John Palmer.

As 1864 came to a close, both Joshua and James Speed went through political changes in their lives. James Speed helped to form the Unconditional Unionist Party, which stood for the recruitment of black Union soldiers, emancipation, and the re-election of Lincoln. He changed his belief that emancipation should be a state issue and supported federal emancipation. Joshua Speed also changed his outlook on slavery. He originally believed that slavery was a legal right and did not support emancipation, but he changed his stance and joined the radical Unconditional Unionist Party. As historian Gary Williams pointed out, the brothers' support of Lincoln and the preservation of the Union changed their view on slavery.[240] After Lincoln won the election in November 1864, his Attorney General Edward Bates stepped down, and he had to find a new Attorney General. Lincoln decided to reward Joshua Speed with the position, but Joshua was a successful business man in Kentucky and did not want to leave his state, so the honor went to James. James Speed accepted Lincoln's call.

---

239 Roy Basler, *Collected Works of Abraham Lincoln*, Vol. 8, Telegraph from Lincoln to Thomas Bramlette, Nov. 22, 1864. (The Abraham Lincoln Association, 1953).

240 Gary Lee Williams, "James and Joshua Speed: Lincoln's Kentucky Friends," (Ph.D. Dissertation, Duke University, 1971), 138.

Chapter Eleven

James Becomes Attorney General

When James Speed took the position of Attorney General, he took on a great responsibility in advising the President on legal matters facing the nation, served as chief of the law officers of the federal government, in which he supervised or represented the United States in any Supreme Court cases, and served as the chief administrator of the federal court system, instructing U.S. district attorneys, marshals, etc.[241] He had to deal with draft laws, reparations laws, confiscation laws, and many other issues dealing with the war. Lincoln wanted a Southern man to serve on his cabinet, but Washington saw a Kentucky lawyer. Only time would tell if James Speed could perform his duties to the satisfaction of the nation.

On November 24, 1864, Attorney General Edward Bates informed Lincoln that he would resign his office. Lincoln needed to find a replacement. He asked Joseph Holt if he would take the position of Attorney General, but Holt wrote to Lincoln that after careful consideration, he could not accept the position. Holt recommended James Speed, stating that "I can recall no public man in the State, of uncompromising loyalty, who unites in the same degree, the qualifications of professional attainments, fervent devotion to the Union, and to the principles of your administration and spotless points of personal character. To these he adds—what I should deem indispensable—a warm & hearty friendship for yourself, personally and officially."[242] On December 1, 1864, Lincoln sent an urgent telegram to James Speed at his home in Louisville. While James Speed sat before

241 Gary Lee Williams, "James and Joshua Speed: Lincoln's Kentucky Friends," (Ph.D. Dissertation, Duke University, 1971), 143.

242 Roy Basler, ed., Collected Works of Abraham Lincoln, Vol. 8, Lincoln to James Speed, December 1, 1864. (The Abraham Lincoln Association, 1953, www.hti.umich.edu), 127; Joseph Holt to Abraham Lincoln, Dec. 1, 1864, The Abraham Lincoln Papers, The Library of Congress, Washington, D.C.

a blazing fire in his office in Louisville, a telegram was handed to him. For a moment, James Speed could not take his mind off his other important papers, which he was reading in one of the suits brought by the Louisville & Nashville Railroad. The telegram was from Lincoln, informing him that Edward Bates had resigned as Attorney General and that Lincoln appointed James Speed to the position. At the end of the telegram, Lincoln wrote: "Please come on at once."[243] James Speed replied: "Will leave tomorrow for Washington."[244] Lincoln told his advisors that he did not know James as well as Joshua Speed, but he stated that James Speed was an "honest man and a gentleman, and if he comes here you will find he is one of those well poised men, not too common here, who are not spoiled by a big office."[245]

Before James Speed left for Washington, Lincoln asked Joshua and James if they had inquired into the case of C.T. Smith and John H. Schramme, who were confined at Rock Island, Illinois, Prison and whether James and Joshua thought that either of Smith or Schramme should be released. Lincoln wrote to James and Joshua that if they persuaded Smith and Schramme to take the oath, he would release the men. Joshua Speed endorsed Lincoln's letter and wrote that he inquired into the character of Smith and Schramme and agreed with their release. Joshua wrote: "The prisoners are also men of heretofore good character—are truly penitent and would from all the information I can get—give willing obedience to the law—and whatever influence they may have in favor of the Government."[246]

According to historian Helen Springer, Lincoln offered the Attorney General's office to James Guthrie. Joshua Speed delivered the letter from Lincoln to Guthrie, but Guthrie told Joshua that his position remained as president of the Louisville and Nashville Railroad. Lincoln called for Joshua Speed to come to Chicago for his inauguration. The President may have offered Joshua the position of Attorney General, but Joshua turned Lincoln down because he was a successful businessman, as proprietor of the Short Line Railroad,

---

243 Basler, *Collected Works of Abraham Lincoln*, Vol. 8, Lincoln to James Speed, December 1, 1864; James Speed, James Speed: A Personality, (Louisville: J. P. Morton & Company, 1914), 51.

244 Basler, *Collected Works of Abraham Lincoln*, Vol. 8, Lincoln to James Speed, December 1, 1864.

245 Robert Kincaid, *Joshua Fry Speed: Lincoln's Most Intimate Friend*, (Harrogate, Tennessee: Lincoln Memorial University, 1943), 29.

246 Basler, *Collected Works of Abraham Lincoln*, Vol. 8, Lincoln to Joshua and James Speed, December 1, 1864.

director in the company, director in the Louisville and Bardstown Turnpike Company, the Louisville Cement Company, the Savings Bank of Louisville, Talmadge Ice Company, and the Louisville Hotel Company.[247]

On December 5, 1864, James Speed wrote to his mother, Lucy Speed, that he had met President Lincoln and decided to take the position of Attorney General, if his nomination were confirmed by the Senate. James knew that he was on the eve of accepting a very "elevated, dignified, and responsible office."[248] All his friends told him to accept the position. He wrote to his mother that he would work hard and honestly for the "good and the glory" of his country. James informed his mother that the call to be Attorney General came suddenly and unexpectedly. He knew the labor of his office would be great and that the changes he made were sudden and great ones and the responsibilities and labors of the office "even greater than the change I have made."[249] He worried that any mistakes he made would result in the country suffering.

Letters seeking his help arrived to his office. A lady from Philadelphia, who was a native Kentuckian, wrote to James seeking his influence to get her only son in the Naval Academy. Another letter from her sister in Little Rock, Arkansas, arrived telling him that her only son was a Rebel prisoner in Johnson's Island and asked him if he would get a parole. Since James Speed held office, people approached him from all parts of the country claiming they knew him, but he wrote his mother that he did not care to know them. While in Washington, James Speed had to attend the many political dinners given by Senators and Congressmen. During one week in January, James had to attend two dinners, one given by Mr. Jordan, Solicitor of the Treasury, and one by Mr. Hopper, a Congressman from Massachusetts. James felt out of place at the fancy dinners. At Mr. Hooper's party, all the men were dressed in swallow tail tuxedos, except James. In attendance at the party were Chief Justice Salmon Chase, Admiral David Farragut, and Secretary of State William Seward. Several different courses came to table, but James did not recognize anything but the soup, fish, sweetbreads and peas. He did not know

247 Helen Springer, "The Political Career of James Speed," (M.A. Thesis, University of Chicago, Illinois, 1936), 73-74.

248 James Speed, *James Speed: A Personality*, 51-52.

249 Ibid., 53.

how many courses were to be brought to the table, or what courses were going to be brought to the table. The dinners were nothing like the dinners at home at Farmington, such as "jowl and turnip greens, or pig's head and hominy."[250]

When Kentucky discovered that James Speed had become Attorney General, Union newspapers supported the appointment. The *Louisville Daily Union Press* announced: "It is unnecessary to speak in Kentucky of the ability, qualifications, staunch, upright, manly traits of this excellent and eminent gentleman. He has stood fast to his allegiance, and fast to the great principles of universal freedom."[251] The *Daily Union Press* stated that Speed was "one of the best of men."[252] George Prentice, editor of the *Louisville Journal* wrote, "we know his unswerving loyalty, and we are convinced that he is not of that fanatical class which denounced those who supported McClellan as traitors. No more faithful or honest gentleman can be found than James Speed."[253] Many Kentuckians had high expectations for James Speed as Attorney General.

Lincoln did not waste time before he asked for James Speed's opinion. On December 29, 1864, he asked James's opinion regarding naval court-martials. Lincoln asked if the Secretary of Navy or any of his subordinates was bound by law on application of individuals, to furnish copies of records of Naval court-martials and whether the Secretary of the Navy was bound to law to answer to a Commission of a State Court, directing the taking of his testimony, as to the contents of records of naval court-martials. Lincoln was referring to H.D. Stover, who was convicted by court-martial of defrauding the Navy Department while he was a contractor at the Philadelphia Naval Yard. Stover was called as a witness in December 1865 in a trial of Thurlow Weed for libeling George Opdyke. During the trial Opdyke's counsel obtained permission for Navy Secretary of War Gideon Welles to be interrogated and to furnish records concerning Stover's court-martial and conviction. Welles did not want to comply, but Lincoln was swayed by the objections of Secretary of War Seward, who denied that the public papers of any Federal department were subject to the demand of any state court or any court in

250 Ibid., 56.

251 Jennifer Cole, "Semper Eadem: An Interpretation of the Life and Career of James Speed," (M.A. Thesis, University of Louisville, 2003), 49.

252 Cole, 49.

253 *Louisville Journal*, December 5, 1864.

a private suit.[254] James Speed gave his opinion that Naval and other court-martials are not state secrets. He stated that "public and private alike require that the Secretary of the Navy and his subordinate officers should not withhold their testimony with respect to the contents of the records in question when required to give it by the summons of the State Court."[255]

Back in Kentucky, Joshua telegraphed his brother James on January 11, 1865, about General "Burbridge and Frankfort."[256] He informed his brother that he sent communication by mail to President Lincoln about Burbridge and Governor Bramlette. Relations between Governor Thomas Bramlette and General Burbridge soured, and Governor Bramlette demanded Lincoln to relieve General Burbridge of his command. During Governor Thomas Bramlette's annual message to the Kentucky legislature on January 6, 1865, he attacked General Burbridge. In his speech he stated that he had selected General Burbridge to carry out certain agreements, such as preventing unlawful acts growing out of black soldiers' recruitment; agreeing to stop recruiting or drafting in each county as soon as its quota was filled, to confine recruiting to the regularly appointed officers for that service, and removing the recruited blacks to camps of instruction outside the state of Kentucky, "instead of doing so, adopted the most offensive and injurious modes of violating them. . . . He established a system of trade permits in violation of law and to the detriment of the public interests-which, as administered, was a most shameful and corrupt system of partisan political corruption and oppression."[257] He advised the legislature to "collect the facts, showing its corrupt use, and present them to the national authorities, in such form as to secure the abolishment and future prohibition of all such interferences with the lawful and necessary trade of the country." The Governor brought up the hog swindle of the 1864 and stated that Burbridge patronized the swindle which was being carried on by the Commissary Department. Bramlette put an end to the hog swindle, but not before "the farmers had sustained losses to at least $300,000–yet in time to save

254 Abraham Lincoln to James Speed, December 29, 1864 (Requests opinion regarding naval court-martials, The Abraham Lincoln Papers, The Library of Congress, Washington, D.C.

255 James Speed to Abraham Lincoln, January 3, 1865, (Opinion on navy court-martials), The Abraham Lincoln Papers, The Library of Congress, Washington, D.C.

256 J. Speed to Attorney General James Speed, January 11, 1865, The Abraham Lincoln Papers, The Library of Congress, Washington, D.C.

257 Collins, Lewis & Collins, Richard, *History of Kentucky*, Vol. 1 , 1874.,151.

them the loss of over $1,000,000. It is due to the honest farmers of the state that you collate, or provide for so doing, the facts bearing upon this attempted and partially executed fraud, and present them also in connection with the military trade regulations." Bramlette stated that the gravest matter of military outrages occurred when loyal citizens were arrested, imprisoned, and banished without a hearing or without even knowing what charges were put against them. The governor stated that many of the arrests were for partisan political vengeance, and the arrested were forced to pay heavy sums of money for their release and stated that "how the spoils, so infamously extorted, are divided, has not transpired to the public information." The governor recommended that the limitation to actions for malicious arrest and false imprisonment be repealed. He also recommended that the offense of causing or obtaining arrests under malicious or false imprisonment a felony or high misdemeanor.[258] By February 1865, Secretary of War Edwin Stanton relieved Burbridge of command and replaced him with General John Palmer.

On February 15, 1865, Joshua Speed wrote to Lincoln stating that Washington McClean, publisher of the *Cincinnati Enquirer*, wanted to exchange Roger Pryor from Fort Lafayette for Captain Pembroke Lovett of the 5th Kentucky Infantry, U.S. A Virginia lawyer, newspaper editor, and a member of the U.S. House of Representatives, the Confederacy elected Roger Pryor to the Provisional Confederate Congress, but he resigned to accept a commission as a colonel in the Confederate army. Promoted to brigadier general in April of 1862, Pryor resigned his commission in August 1863. Union forces captured Pryor in November 1864, while serving as a special courier under an informal truce. Joshua Speed wanted Captain Pembroke Lovett, of the U.S. 5th Kentucky infantry, exchanged for Pryor. Confederate forces captured Lovett at the Battle of Chickamauga. Lazarus Powell, former Kentucky governor and politician, joined Joshua Speed's petition. Lincoln met with McLean on February 17, 1865, and gave him a note that authorized Secretary of War Edwin Stanton to exchange Pryor.[259] Both Stanton and General Ulysses S. Grant objected, but Lincoln proceeded with Pryor's exchange.[260]

---

258 Ibid., 151.

259 Joshua Speed to Abraham Lincoln, Feb. 15, 1865, The Abraham Lincoln Papers, The Library of Congress, Washington, D.C.

260 John W. Forney to Abraham Lincoln, Feb 18, 1865, The Abraham Lincoln Papers, The Library of Congress, Washington, D.C.

While Attorney General, James Speed wrote 116 opinions. Speed gave his opinion on such topics as the Draft Laws of 1864 and 1865, government confiscation of enemy property, conflicting land claims, bounties to soldiers, violations of the slave trade status, railroad bonds in the West, Native American relations, issue in Panama, Japan and Hawaii, and court-martials.[261]

During the Civil War the South claimed they had belligerent rights, meaning that the United States fought with a government, not individuals, therefore the Confederates could not be held responsible for acts that would otherwise be considered treason. The United States claimed the South was in rebellion and did not fight a belligerent government, but in other cases the United States wished to recognize the rights of the South in prize cases.

In December 1864, James Speed heard the case of the schooner Andromeda. The Union ship the Pursuit captured the Andromeda on May 20, 1862, off the coast of Cuba. At the time, the ship carried cotton and hides and was headed for the Sabine River in Texas. The courts ruled that the cargo aboard the Andromeda was enemy property and liable to seizure by the United States. On June 9, 1862, the United States ship Bainbridge captured the schooner Baigorry, carrying a cargo of cotton, heading for Havana. The courts deemed the ship a prize of war and enemy property.[262]

During May of 1864 Union forces seized 72 bales of cotton on Mrs. Elizabeth Alexander's plantation, located on the Red River. In the spring of 1864, a naval force under Rear Admiral David Porter cooperating with military forces on land, under General Nathaniel Banks, headed up the Red River. Banks and Porter seized 72 bales of cotton in a warehouse, a mile from the river. Union forces sent the cotton to Cairo and the bales were deemed a prize of war. Mrs. Alexander claimed the cotton and the district court ruled that the cotton should be returned to her. The United States asked for a reversal of the decision. Attorney General Speed ruled that the cotton was a lawful maritime prize. Speed argued that the commercial property in enemy country was a lawful prize regardless of loyalty, that commercial property was a lawful prize of war if captured afloat on the Red River by a naval force. He also gave his opinion that if the

261 Cole, "Semper Eadem: An Interpretation of the Life and Career of James Speed," 51; Springer, "The Political Career of James Speed," 78.

262 Springer, "The Political Career of James Speed," 78.

72 bales were deemed enemy commercial property, and if captured in enemy territory by the naval force, then the capture, though made on land, was lawful. In his opinion, Speed ruled that the lower courts should be reversed and the property condemned as a prize of war.[263] Speed lost his contention that Mrs. Alexander's cotton was a lawful maritime prize, because the cotton seized was in territory already occupied by the civil and military authorities. Chief Justice Chase ruled his opinion on the Captured and Abandoned Property Act of March 3, 1863. As the Federal armies advanced, Union soldiers took a great amount of cotton. Under this act, treasury agents took over the captured rebel property, and sold the property in loyal states. Chief Justice Chase stated that the cotton taken from Mrs. Alexander was a lawful capture, but not a maritime prize. He ruled that any claimant could bring suit against the government two years after the war ended. In his opinion, the cotton should have been turned over the Treasury Department, and not a maritime prize.[264]

As Attorney General, James Speed gave his opinion on the conscription laws of 1864 and 1865. The draft of 1864 permitted the drafted person to hire a substitute and would not be subject to any subsequent draft law. The conscription law of 1864 dropped the payment of commutation money. James Speed stated that the substitute served three years and remained liable to the draft and the principal was insured against the risk of being drafted during the whole period for the substitute's enlistment. A year later, the government tried to encourage volunteering and advised communities to organize recruiting societies to induce volunteers to enlist before the draft and pay the enlistees a bounty. Speed stated that there was no conflict between the conscription acts of 1864 and 1865. A citizen liable to the draft had the alternative course to pursue before any draft, either to buy a substitute and secure him to be mustered in and obtain an exemption from the draft during the entire term of enlistment of the substitute, or he could procure for the government a recruit not liable to the draft, and obtain credit for the recruit in case he should be drafted, substituting himself to the liability of being compelled to repeat the operation at every succeeding draft that may be ordered by the President.[265] Secretary of War Edwin Stanton asked James

263 Ibid., 80.
264 Ibid., 80-81.
265 Ibid., 83-84.

Speed's opinion on whether the recruits which were to be taken as substitutes were to be considered as other volunteer recruits or as substitutes which were furnished at the cost of the principals. Speed stated that the men were to be considered as other volunteer recruits, not as substitutes.[266]

On December 19, 1864, Lincoln called for another 300,000 volunteers. On January 24, 1865, the War Department assigned each state their quota of volunteers. James Speed gave his opinion on the legal points on the enrollment act. James Speed stated that Congress desired the draft should be equalized among the population of the several states. The United States was divided into districts; each territory would constitute one or more and each congressional district of the states as fixed by a law of the state next preceding the enrolment, would constitute one. The board of enrollment would be in each district. James Speed gave his opinion that the mode of ascertaining and assigning to states and districts their respective quotas as prescribed in the act of July 3, 1863, was not repealed and that the same mode must be pursued in equalizing the draft among the subdivisions of each district. James Speed wrote to the President that the words "period of time" in the enrolment act of 1864 and "time of service" used in the March 3, 1863 meant the same thing. He also recommended that the President must give credit by the whole period or term for which the man enlisted.[267] If a state did not fill their quota of volunteers by February 15, the difference had to be made up by the draft. Officials in several states claimed that the formulas used by the War Department to calculate the quotas were unfair. The governors of New York, Rhode Island, Massachusetts, and Vermont urged Lincoln to ameliorate the situation. On February 6, Lincoln signed an order that created a board to examine the quotas and appointed James Speed, General Richard Delafield and Colonel Charles W. Foster to the board, with Speed acting president of the board.[268]

As the months passed by, James Speed dealt with the many issues facing the nation, such as draft laws, confiscation laws, and

266 Ibid.

267 James Speed to Abraham Lincoln, Feb. 9, 1865 (Opinion on conscription in response to letter by Andrew G. Curtin), The Abraham Lincoln Papers, The Library of Congress, Washington, D.C.

268 Abraham Lincoln to John Gregory Smith, February 8, 1865, The Abraham Lincoln Papers, The Library of Congress, Washington, D.C. Translated and Annotated by the Lincoln Studies Center, Knox College, Galesburg, Illinois.

gave his legal opinion to the president. James Speed must have felt overwhelmed with the horde of Kentuckians asking for favors, the political dealings in Washington, and the massive work load, but all his work to date would pale in comparison to the greatest loss to the nation: the assassination of Lincoln. Lincoln's death would have a profound effect upon James and Joshua Speed's lives. James Speed would have to deal with new issues and challenges as Attorney General in dealing with assassins, and Joshua Speed would have to deal with the loss of his best friend.

Chapter Twelve

The Death of Lincoln

In April 1865, Joshua and James Speed and the nation would have to deal with the death of Abraham Lincoln. James not only lost a friend, but he would have to deal as Attorney General with new issues and legal opinions concerning the capture and trial of the assassins. Joshua had to deal with not only the loss of his President, but also the loss of his best friend. The loss of Lincoln touched all of the Speeds, including Lucy. James and Joshua made sure they would carry on Lincoln's legacy.

During the early part of April, Lincoln asked James to ask his brother Joshua to pay him a visit before Joshua went back home to Kentucky. Joshua arrived at the White House to see Lincoln and found him "jaded and weary." Joshua stayed in the room until his hour for visitors was over. Lincoln then ordered the door closed and, looking over to where Joshua was seated, asked him to come closer to his chair. Instead of being alone, in the opposite direction from where Joshua sat, and across the fire-place from Lincoln, sat two women. Lincoln saw the two women and said: "Well, ladies, what can I do for you?" One of the women was old, the other young. They both talked at once, and the President comprehended what they were saying to him. He then said: "I suppose that your son and your husband are in prison for resisting the draft in Western Pennsylvania. Where is your petition?" The old lady replied, "Mr. Lincoln, I've got no petition, I went to a lawyer to get one drawn, and I had not the money to pay him and come here too; so I thought I would just come and ask you to let me have my boy." Lincoln turned to the young woman and replied: "And it's your husband you want?" She said "Yes." Lincoln rang his bell and called his servant and told him to go tell General Dana to bring him the list of prisoners for resisting the draft in western Pennsylvania. The General came and brought a package of papers. The President opened the package and counting the names said, "General, there are 27 of these men. Is there any difference in degree of their guilt?" General Dana replied "No, it is a bad case, and a merciful finding." Lincoln, looking out the window and talking to himself, said: "Well, these poor fellows have, I think, suffered enough; they have been in prison 15 months. I have been thinking so for some time, and have so said to Stanton, and he always threatened to resign if they are released. But he has said so about other matters, and never did. So now, while I have the paper in hand, I will turn out the flock." He wrote on the paper, "Let the prisoners named in the within paper be discharged" and signed the paper. The General took the paper and left the office. Then, turning to the ladies he said, "Now, ladies, you can go. Your son, madam, and your husband, madam, are free." The young woman ran across the room and knelt before Lincoln. He took her by the elbow and said, impatiently, "Get up, get up, none of this." But the old woman walked to him, wiping with her apron the tears that ran down her cheeks. She gave him her hand, and looking into his face said: "Good-bye, Mr. Lincoln; we will never meet again till we meet in Heaven." A change came over Lincoln's "sad and weary" face. He clasped her hand in both of his and followed her to the door, saying as he went, "With all that I have to cross me here, I am afraid that I will never get there, but your wish that you will meet me there has fully paid for all I have done for you."[269]

After the women left, Joshua and Lincoln were alone in the room. Lincoln drew his chair to the fire and said, "Speed, I am a little alarmed about myself; just feel my hand." Joshua Speed felt Lincoln's hand; which was cold and clammy. Lincoln pulled off his boots and put his feet to the fire, which made his feet steam. Joshua told Lincoln he was overworked. Lincoln replied, "No, I am not tired." Joshua Speed said: "Such a scene as I have just witnessed is enough to make you nervous." Lincoln replied: "How much you are mistaken. I have made two people happy today; I have given a mother her son, and a wife her husband. That young woman is a counterfeit, but the old woman is a true mother."[270] This would be the last time Joshua Speed would see his old friend.

On April 9, 1865, Confederate General Robert E. Lee surrendered to Union General Ulysses S. Grant at Appomattox Courthouse,

269 Joshua Fry Speed, *Reminiscences of Abraham Lincoln and Notes of a Visit to California*, two lectures. (Louisville, Kentucky, Bradley & Gilbert & Co., 1896), 27-28.

270 Ibid.

Virginia. The Radical Republicans did not like the lenient conditions that General Grant gave to General Lee. In Kentucky, members such as Rev. Robert Breckinridge and the Radical members drew James Speed into the Radical movement. Radicals in Lincoln's cabinet, such as Charles Sumner, Edwin Stanton, Chief Justice Chase and Dennison, drew James Speed into their wing. James Speed argued with Lincoln over his decision to allow the Virginia Legislature to vote to restore Virginia to the Union. He thought Lincoln was lenient to the southerners and did not agree with Lincoln's peace initiatives. Speed told Chief Justice Chase that after a cabinet meeting with Lincoln, he "made a mistake at Richmond in sanctioning the assembling of the Virginia Legislature; and had perhaps been too fast in his desire for early reconstruction."[271] On April 10, 1865, James Speed changed his opinion after he visited Richmond, Virginia. He described the business section of Richmond in ruins. The white people looked dejected and subdued. James wrote his mother that he could have "wept from pure sympathy."[272] So strong was James's sympathy that he almost forgot that the people of Richmond were reaping "the fruits of the trees they had planted." He stated that after seeing the devastation of Richmond, his future notions and conduct would be greatly modified.

On April 15, 1865, John Wilkes Booth shot President Abraham Lincoln at Ford's Theater. After the shooting, doctors and military personnel took Lincoln to Mr. Peterson's house across the street. Secretary of the Navy Gideon Welles kept a diary of the events which took place when he and Secretary of War Edwin Stanton arrived at the Peterson house. When Stanton and Welles arrived, they entered the Peterson House, ascended a flight of steps above the basement and passed through the hall to the rear. The President lay on a bed, breathing heavily. Several surgeons were present. Welles asked Doctor Hall the true condition of the president. He told Welles that the President was "dead to all intents, although he might live three hours or perhaps longer."[273] Lincoln lay diagonally across the bed. He had

---

271 Helen Springer, "The Political Career of James Speed," (M.A. Thesis, University of Chicago, Illinois, 1936), 85.

272 James Speed, *James Speed: A Personality*, (Louisville: J. P. Morton & Company, 1914), 59.

273 Welles, Gideon, *Diary of Gideon Welles: Secretary of the Navy under Lincoln and Johnson*, with an introduction by John T. Morse, Jr. Vol. II, (Boston and New York: Houghton Mifflin Company, 1911)

been stripped of his clothes. His slow, full respiration, lifted the blanket with each breath. Lincoln's right eye began to swell from the bullet lodged behind his eye and his face became discolored. When Welles entered the room Secretary Charles Sumner, Speaker Schuyler Colfax, Secretary of the Treasury Hugh McCulloch, and other members of the cabinet, except Secretary of State William Seward, sat near Lincoln's bed. The room quickly became overcrowded. The hall and other rooms in the front or main house overflowed with people. One of the rooms was occupied by Mary Todd Lincoln and her attendants. Once an hour Mrs. Lincoln would sit next to her husband's bedside. She cried hysterically until the cabinet members had to remove her.

On April 15, a door which opened upon a porch or gallery, and the windows, were kept open for fresh air. At 6:00 a.m., Welles left the room and went for a walk. When he returned to the Peterson's parlor, James Speed and others were taking evidence concerning the assassination. At 7:00 a.m., Welles entered Lincoln's room. Mrs. Lincoln and Robert Lincoln stood watching Abraham Lincoln's last moments on earth. Robert Lincoln at one point became overwhelmed with grief and cried on Senator Sumner's shoulder. Lincoln took his last breath at 7:22 a.m. A prayer followed from Dr. Gurley, and the cabinet, with the exception of Secretary Seward and Secretary McCulloch, assembled in the back parlor and signed a letter which was prepared by James Speed to the vice president.[274]

James Speed's letter advised Andrew Johnson, Lincoln's vice president, that with the death of Lincoln, the office of President devolved under the Constitution to Johnson. James Speed, along with McCulloch, took his letter to the Kirkwood House, where they met Chief Justice Salmon Chase and informed him they were on their way to his house to ask him to administer the oath to the new president. Chase, along with James Speed discussed the precedents and examined the constitution and laws concerning vice presidents becoming presidents. After examining the precedents and the Constitution, they returned to the hotel. With 14 other men, who assembled in the hotel, Chase had Johnson repeat the oath to become the new president of the United States. After taking the oath, Johnson told Speed and McCulloch to remain in the room. Johnson assured the

274 Ibid.

men in the room that he needed the present cabinet to help him in his difficult times.[275] Although James Speed wanted to keep his job as Attorney General, he and the rest of the cabinet already had a bad first impression of Johnson. During his inauguration speech, on March 4, 1865, Johnson made a long, blustering, rambling speech, and many of the cabinet members thought he was under the influence of alcohol. At one point, James leaned over to Gideon Welles, and whispered, "All this is in wretched bad taste. The man is certainly deranged."[276] Recovering from typhoid fever at the time, Johnson had drunk some whiskey to steady his nerves before his inaugural speech, but the whiskey only unsteadied them, resulting in his rambling speech.[277] Johnson also did not have a high opinion of James Speed. President Johnson commented to his private secretary that James was a man of no great consequence and stated that Speed's wife was the better man of the two.[278] The relationship between President Johnson and Attorney General James Speed would not improve during Johnson's administration.

Within hours after Lincoln's assassination, the entire government focused on capturing the assassins. Federal troops searched Maryland for John Wilkes Booth and his accomplices. On April 17, Federal agents captured several suspects at the boardinghouse of Mary Surratt, including Mrs. Surratt and Lewis Payne. On that same day, Federal troops arrested Samuel Arnold, who was a former schoolmate of Booth's and a Confederate veteran; Michael O'Laughlin, another of Booth's boyhood friends; and Edman Spangler, who held the reins of Booth's horse at Ford's theater. On April 20, Federal troops arrested George Atzerodt. On April 24, 1865, Federal troops arrested Dr. Samuel Mudd, who treated Booth's leg and allowed Booth and David Herold to stay overnight.[279]

James Speed and Secretary of War Stanton agreed that Judge

---

275 Ibid.

276 Ibid.

277 Springer, "The Political Career of James Speed," 87; Gary Lee Williams, "James and Joshua Speed: Lincoln's Kentucky Friends," (Ph.D. Dissertation, Duke University, 1971), 153; Jennifer Cole, "Semper Eadem: An Interpretation of the Life and Career of James Speed," 53; Hans Trefousse, *Andrew Johnson: A Biography*, (New York & London: W. W. Norton & Company, 1989), 194.

278 Hans Trefousse, *Andrew Johnson: A Biography*, 208.

279 James Swanson & Daniel Weinberg, *Lincoln's Assassins: Their Trial and Execution*, Arena Editions, 2001.

Advocate General Joseph Holt should be placed in charge of the investigation into the conspiracy that Booth may have been working with the Confederate government in the assassination of Lincoln. On April 26, Federal soldiers caught up with Booth at the Garrett farm and killed him. David Herold surrendered to Federal authorities at the Garrett's farm before Federal troops set the barn containing Booth on fire. By the end of April, Holt collected enough evidence to convince Johnson and Stanton that high Southern officials including Confederate President Jefferson Davis had taken part in Lincoln's assassination.[280]

After Lincoln's death, James Speed wrote to his mother that the best man he ever knew and "one holding just now the highest and most responsible position on earth, had been taken from us, but do not be downcast and hopeless." James Speed had hope and faith that the Government would not be bound up in the life of any one man. James Speed realized that now the President was dead, he hoped that he would be able to perform his duty and his whole duty to the country. The death of the President would increase his labors and responsibilities.[281] When Lucy Speed heard the news that Lincoln had been assassinated, she was so shocked she was speechless for several moments then she said: "If it had been my son, James, the news would not wound me more."[282]

On April 19, 1865, Joshua sat with a sad heart in a called meeting of the citizens of Louisville to mourn the President's death and to draft resolutions to send to President Andrew Johnson, pledging their faith and loyalty. The committee named Joshua Speed vice president of the meeting and assigned him to assist in the arrangements for a memorial service for Lincoln.[283]

By April 20, James continued to soften his heart toward the southerners. He wrote to his mother that the nation must show "mercy, charity, and forgiveness to those who have wildly and madly sinned. How much sweeter duty than that of slaughtering them with the terrible engines of war." He also stated that the "seeds of mercy and forgiveness" that the nation planted would bring the "sweet

280 Williams, 155.

281 James Speed, *James Speed: A Personality*, 59-60.

282 Robert Kincaid, *Joshua Speed: Lincoln's Most Intimate Friend*, (Harrogate, Tennessee: Lincoln Memorial University, 1943), 29.

283 Ibid. 29.

blossoms and life giving fruits of peace." He promised that "love shall overcome hate."[284]

On April 22, 1865, James Speed dealt with the surrender of the Confederate army of Northern Virginia. Stanton asked Speed if the former Confederate soldiers from the Army of Northern Virginia who lived in the city of Washington before the war could return to their homes. Speed stated that the rebel officers who surrendered to Union General Ulysses S. Grant have no homes within the loyal states and have no right to come to places which were their homes prior to their going into the rebellion. He also stated that anyone in the civil service of the rebellion had no right to return to Washington. Speed informed Stanton that rebel officers had no right to wear their uniforms in any of the loyal states. He felt that the former Confederate officers only added insult to injury when they wore their uniforms in the streets and considered the wearing of Confederate uniforms an act of hostility against the government.[285]

By late April 1865, the nation prepared for the trial of Booth's accomplices. The question before the President and his cabinet was whether to try the conspirators in a civilian court or a military court. Edwin Stanton, Andrew Johnson, and Joseph Holt wanted a military trial, but Secretary of the Navy Gideon Welles and Secretary of the Treasury Hugh McCulloch wanted a civilian trial. The President turned to James Speed for the final say in the matter. On April 28, 1865, James wrote to the President, "Sir, I am of the opinion that the persons charged with the murder of the President of the United States can be rightfully tried by a military court." Former Attorney General Edward Bates opposed the military commission, stating that the proceedings were unlawful. In his diary he wrote that on May 12, 1865, he received the *Philadelphia Public Ledge*r on the "Secret Military Tribunals" and a reprint of the May 11, 1865, editorial from the *New York Tribune* on the same subject. He also received the *New York Post*, the *New York Tribune* and the *New York Times*, which came out against the trial of the assassins of the President and the attempted murder of Seward, by a military commission. He wrote in his diary:

> I am pained to be led to believe that my successor, Attorney General Speed, has been wheeled out of an

284 James Speed, *James Speed: A Personality*, 61.
285 Springer, "The Political Career of James Speed," 99.

> opinion, to the effect that such a trial is lawful. If he be, in the lowest degree, qualified for his office, he must know better. Such a trial is not only unlawful, but it is a gross blunder in policy: It denies the great, fundamental principle, that ours is a government of Law, and that the law is strong enough, to rule the people wisely and well; and if the offenders be done to death by that tribunal, however truly guilty, they will pass for martyrs with half the world.[286]

Bates believed that James Speed's ruling on trying the military conspirators in a military court was the working of Stanton.

On May 1, President Johnson took Speed's advice and ordered a military trial of the Lincoln assassins. The President ordered a nine-man military commission to preside over the trial of the assassins. The nine men were Major Generals David Hunter and Lewis Wallace, Brevet Major General August V. Kautz, Brigadier Generals Albion Howe, R.S. Foster, and Thomas M. Harris, Brevet Brigadier General James A. Ekin, Brevet Colonel Charles H. Tompkins, and Lieutenant Colonel David Clendenin. The courtroom for the nine-man commission held session in the Old Penitentiary. The commission heard evidence from May 10 through June 29, 1865. Over the course of seven weeks, the military commission took the testimony of 361 witnesses and compiled a transcript containing 4,900 pages. On June 29, the military commission deliberated in secret to review the evidence. After deliberation, the commission sentenced four of the conspirators to be hanged: Lewis Powell, Mary Surratt, David Herold, and George Atzerodt. On July 5, 1865, the commission presented their verdicts and sentences to President Johnson. With the announcement that Mrs. Surratt was to be hanged, many Americans could not believe that the government would hang a woman. The government did not allow the defendants legal appeals or time to seek clemency from the President. Surratt's attorney's John W. Clampitt and Frederick W. Aiken drafted legal papers to try and save Mary Surratt. At the White House, Surratt's daughter, Anna Surratt and others tried to see President Johnson to beg for Mary Surratt's life, but he refused to see them. On July 7, Surratt's attorney's won a writ of habeas

286 Beale, Howard, ed, *The Diary of Edward Bates: 1858-1866*, (Washington: D.C.: Government Printing Office, 1933), 483.

corpus from a civil court, ordering her release from military custody. Clampitt gave the writ to the United States marshal at 4:00 a.m. on July 7 to be served on General Hancock. At 10:00 a.m., President Johnson wrote a note to General Hancock stating that he declared the writ of habeas corpus suspended and directed Hancock to proceed to execute the order given by the military commission. At noon, General Hancock and James Speed rushed to court with President Johnson's executive order suspending the writ. Five of the judges of the commission signed a document asking Johnson to commute Surratt's sentence to life in prison.[287] But there was no clemency for Mary Surratt, on July 7, 1865, the government carried out the sentence and hanged David E. Herold, G.A. Atzerodt, Lewis Payne, and Mary Surratt.

During the month of June 1865, Joshua and Fanny Speed were among 60 members of the Speed family in Kentucky who subscribed a dollar each to the National Lincoln Monument Association, in order to raise enough money to build a monument for Lincoln's tomb in Springfield, Illinois. Heading the list was Lucy Speed and Joshua's half sister, Mary and Eliza. The monument would cost $200,000. The states of Illinois, Missouri, New York, and Nevada contributed $61,500 towards the monument.[288]

In July after the executions, James Speed wrote his opinion as Attorney General on whether the persons charged with the offense of having assassinated the President could be tried before a military tribunal, or in a civilian court. According to historian Gary Williams, the opinion may have been written by the urging of Stanton or Johnson because of the public criticism of the military trial. Williams wrote, "The opinion was a justification after the fact."[289] According to James Speed, at the time of the assassination, the city of Washington was defended by fortifications, and the principal police in the city were federal soldiers, and President Lincoln, along with the White House, was guarded by soldiers. Marital law had been declared in the District of Columbia. He wrote that military tribunals existed under and according to the laws and usages of war in the interest of

287 Swanson & Weinberg, *Lincoln's Assassins: Their Trial and Execution*, 25-26; Moore, Guy, *The Case of Mrs. Surratt: Her Controversial Trial and Execution for Conspiracy in the Lincoln Assassination*, (Norman: University of Oklahoma Press, 1954), 58.

288 Robert Kincaid, *Joshua Fry Speed: Lincoln's Most Intimate Friend*, 29; Joshua Speed, *Reminiscences of Abraham Lincoln & Notes of a Visit to California: two lectures with a sketch of his life*, (Louisville: Bradley & Gilbert Company, 1896), 42.

289 Gary Lee Williams, "James and Joshua Speed: Lincoln's Kentucky Friends," 159.

justice and mercy. In all wars, and especially in civil wars, secret but active enemies were almost as numerous as open ones. The laws of war authorized commanders to create and establish military commissions, courts, or tribunals for the trial of offenders against the laws of war, whether they were active or secret participants in the hostilities. Obedience to the constitution and the law required that the military should do their whole duty. The military should fight the enemies of the country in open battle, but they must kill or take the secret enemies of the country and try and execute them according to the laws of war. He concluded that Booth and his associates were secret active public enemies. Speed also stated that since Booth yelled out "Sic Semper Tyrannis" after shooting Lincoln and his dying message to his mother that he had died for his country only showed that he was not an assassin from public malice, but acted as a public enemy. Speed concluded that if "the persons who are charged with the assassination of the President committed the deed as public enemies, as I believe they did, and whether they did or not is a question to be decided by the tribunal before which they are tried, they not only can but ought to be tried before a military tribunal. If the persons charged have offended against the laws of war, it would be as palpably wrong for the military to hand them over to the civilian courts, as it would be wrong in a civilian court to convict a man of murder who had, in time of war, killed another in battle."[290]

Not everyone agreed with Speed's opinion and his arguments. Former Attorney General Edward Bates wrote a scathing review of Speed's opinion allowing a military trial of the assassins:

> This is the most extraordinary document I ever read, under the name of a law opinion. The opinion is addressed to the President and dated "July ---1865." After the sentence, and in fact, after the execution of the accused, who were condemned to death! And thus, it is apparent that the opinion was gotten up (a mere fetch of the War office) to bolster up a jurisdiction,

290 James Speed, "Opinion on the constitutional power of the Military to try and execute the Assassins of the President," (Washington, D.C.: Government Printing Office, 1865), Springer, 92; Cole, 56.

> after the fact, so generally denounced by lawyers and by the respectable Press all over the country."[291]

Bates analyzed and argued Speed's opinion. Bates stated that treason can be committed only by a public enemy, because treason consists only "in levying war against the U.S. or adhering to their enemies, giving them aid or comfort." He stated that pirates were also public enemies, but following Speed's argument, they can be tried lawfully only by a military tribunal. According to Bates, with Speed's argument, "the only question (to give jurisdiction) is did the offender act as a public enemy, or only of his private malice—If the former, the military must try, that being the general, public government, and the Civil Courts being designed only to punish private offenders and redress private wrongs!"[292]

Bates also stated that Speed did not call his military tribunals by the name of military courts nor did he pretend that there was any written law for a military tribunal. Military tribunals are not court-martials, which were created, limited, and governed by the act of Congress, but created by a commander, with no rule for their constitution, whether they consisted of one or many, of officers or privates, with no limit as to the kind of cases to be tried except that the accused must be public enemies and no legal forms of trial; and no designation of the kind and degree of punishment to be awarded. The Constitution states that there can be no "cruel and unusual punishment," but the law does not apply to military tribunals under the laws of war. Bates agued that there was no known law for a military tribunal's existence and that "there can be no prescribed form for their creation and mode of action, and no written limitation of their powers."[293] Bates agreed with Speed that the military tribunal was unlimited as to the sentence they may produce, but the sentence has no force until approved by the President. The military commission had no power to execute their sentence; but the President could annul the sentence. Bates stated there was no such thing as laws of war. "War is the very reverse of Law and its existence always implies (as between the parties to the war) the absence or disregard of all law."[294]

291 Beale, Howard, ed., *The Diary of Edward Bates: 1859-1866*, (Washington, D.C.: Government Printing Office, 1933), 499.

292 Ibid, 500.

293 Ibid, 500.

294 Ibid, 501.

As Attorney General, James Speed worked closely with Johnson on such issues as the Confiscation Acts, pardons, and treason. In May 1865, Speed instructed district attorneys general to stop confiscation proceedings. His order was revoked and the government attorneys were instructed to begin new prosecutions. The Radicals wanted to punish southerners, especially the leaders. Secretary of the Treasury Hugh McCulloch asked Speed whether he could prevent the firm of G. Wheelwright and Company of New York from purchasing cotton, naval stores, and tobacco from citizens in North Carolina who participated in the rebellion and had not been pardoned. Under the Confiscation Act of 1862, the property of Confederate citizens could be confiscated. Speed gave his opinion that northern merchants could not acquire property unless the President pardoned the sellers of the property. In late July, Speed began to restrict enforcement of the Confiscation Acts. In December 1865, Speed ordered the United States Attorney General for Florida to stop the sale of confiscated land as well as the confiscated railroads. He also ordered that confiscation laws could not seize corporate property. Confiscation proceedings and treason rarely led to prosecution and convictions. By the spring of 1866, Speed reversed his policy and advised that the Confiscation Act of July 17, 1862, was a war measure and expired with the war. On April 24, 1866, Speed ruled that 340 bales of cotton, belonging to Joseph P. Billups, should be restored to the owner.

Speed wrote an opinion for Johnson on the power of the President to pardon offenses against the United States. James Speed informed Johnson that the power to pardon individuals and whole classes of persons lay solely in the hands of the President. He advised the President to issue another amnesty proclamation. The new amnesty policy would include more exceptions than Lincoln's previous amnesty proclamation. He thought that certain Southern leaders should be denied immediate clemency. Speed advised the President to give mercy upon the great masses of the misguided people in order to reorganize society upon a loyal and freedom-loving basis. He concluded that the South must be restored, not reconstructed. On May 9, James Speed wrote his opinion on the pardoning power and his amnesty proclamation. On May 29, Johnson issued his amnesty proclamation. Any former Confederate who swore allegiance to the Constitution and the Union gained a general pardon. Fourteen classes of people were exempted from the general pardon, including certain Confederate civil and military officers, all who had taken and violated the amnesty oath and all rebels who owned more than $20,000 worth of taxable property. The wealthy and Confederate officers had to apply for a special pardon through the Attorney General's office. The special pardon contained a provision that the person accepted the constitutionality and legality of the emancipation proclamation. On July 20, 1865, James Speed received 150 applications for pardon and a month later, 25,000 applications for pardon arrived at Speed's desk. On September 10, 1865, James Speed wrote home to his mother that he had seen a great many men from the South asking for pardons. He wrote that many of the southerners wanted to come back to the Union. Speed stated that he believed that the "spirit of love will soon roll back the dark and terrible clouds that have hung over and about us. . . May the day soon come throughout this land we shall be all brothers. My desire is to aid in accomplishing that, my labor to find out the way to do it."[295]

On May 9, 1865, Johnson's cabinet discussed North Carolina's reconstruction. Johnson issued the North Carolina Proclamation stating that there was no need for black suffrage and by July 13, 1865, proclamations appointing provisional governors and the plans of procedure to establish loyal governments were issued to all the unreconstructed states. Johnson felt that suffrage was a state matter. James Speed convinced himself that the black man must be given suffrage rights. He was a radical in the sense that he not only wanted to end slavery, but also wanted to make sure that the black man would attain political and civil equality. James Speed wrote to Senator Charles Sumner that the federal government had a right to make local governments for the people of the disloyal states. As long as the disloyal states are enemies and hostile to the government, the United States government had the right to control them, but when the disloyal states laid down their arms and ceased hostility, then they must make their own governments. The United States government could not make their governments and could not dictate to them. According to James Speed, the southern states would be readmitted after the people remade their governments. The people consisted of blacks and whites. So long as the black man was given political rights, the southern states would have no problems being readmitted in the

295 James Speed, *James Speed: A Personality*, 65-66

Union. As historian Gary Williams pointed out, James Speed was not for Congressional control of reconstruction, but wanted black participation in the process. James Speed wrote to his brother on the subject of black suffrage.[296] With the current antagonisms among the different political parties and under current laws of the Constitution, he did not see how the government could do anything about the subject of black suffrage. He thought that the right to secede on the part of the state was just as absurd as the notion that the government had the right to claim control over the status of suffrage in the States.[297]

As for the President, James Speed had a high opinion of the President. He wrote to his brother Joshua that the President "is a remarkable man. I have seen him intimately since he went into his great office, and can say with confidence that he is a patriot and as unselfish as Mr. Lincoln was. Mr. Lincoln made mistakes, but he was honest and the country and the world forgave him. Mr. Johnson may make mistakes, but if he does they will be unselfish and he will be honest."[298] During the month of October, James Speed continued to meet with southerners asking for pardons. A rebel governor from a rebel state came to see James Speed seeking a pardon. After a short, official and formal interview, James Speed sent a recommendation to the President to pardon the Rebel. After receiving his pardon from the President, the rebel governor came running to James Speed out of breath and "wild with joy." He thanked James Speed and James Speed wrote to his mother that he was "thankful for this good time coming."[299]

By December 1865, James Speed continued to give special pardons to a great number of southerners. He stated that the southerners would never own any property in slaves or make use of slave labor. Their hired servants and employees must be free people. When the southern states had to give up slavery in order to receive a pardon, he stated that some of the Virginians and South Carolinians "gag awfully when the pill is first presented, but so far none have refused to take it, and, without exception, after it has been swallowed, they improve rapidly. It seems to renew their sight and the present and future look much brighter than ever before."[300]

---

296 Gary Lee Williams, "James and Joshua Speed: Lincoln's Kentucky Friends," 187.
297 James Speed, *James Speed: A Personality*, 66-67.
298 Ibid. 69.
299 Ibid,. 70-71.
300 Ibid. 75.

On December 25, 1865, James Speed read the Louisville newspapers and Kentucky's anti-construction actions and hoped that Kentucky would give up her stance on slavery:

> Kentucky seems to know less than a blind puppy that has the sense to find the mother's teat and not to wound it. Kentucky hangs on to the teat, but with the fierceness of a tiger growls and scratches all the time. Fortunately, she cuts herself; trying to, in her madness, to injure the General Government, she is making ugly sores upon her own body, and future history will not let the scar disappear. . . [Kentucky] had her hand in the death wound of the monster of slavery, the last desperate struggles of the hideous creature have been upon her soil, and yet she is unbelieving. Poor Kentucky![301]

As the year came to a close, James Speed looked back as his role as Attorney General. He wrote to his mother that "Great questions and great events of great moment to the country and to mankind and with the shaping of which I have more or less to do, so crowd upon one another that there is not time for stately and solemn funerals over the dead past. On we must go, and it would be as silly to go forward in the dark with the lantern behind as to be thinking and dreaming of the past just now. . . I am in for the new year and nerved to the work it brings and ever hopeful that an honest and intelligent discharge of duty will, under God, yield pleasant and healthful fruit."[302]

As 1865 came to an end, James and his brother Joshua had to deal with the loss of their friend and President Abraham Lincoln. James Speed dealt with the Lincoln conspirators, which brought him grief. He had to deal with the end of the war, and reconstruction. James Speed admired President Johnson, but the amicable relationship between the president and his attorney general would come to an end over black equality. James Speed became a radical member in Johnson's administration over black equality and the President would not tolerate Speed and his policies.

301 Ibid. 77.
302 Ibid. 79.

Chapter Thirteen

The Trial of Jefferson Davis

By January 1866, James Speed and President Andrew Johnson worked together on reconstruction, but issues dealing with black suffrage and equality would soon bring a rupture between the two men. James Speed became a radical member in Johnson's cabinet over black suffrage. Also during Johnson's administration, James Speed had to deal with what to do with Confederate President Jefferson Davis and the Fenian movement.

During the month of January 1866, the Senate introduced a bill to renew the Freedman's Bureau by Republican Lyman Trumbull. Congress designed the Freedman's Bureau as a relief agency for destitute blacks and expired on March 3, 1866, unless Congress renewed the bill. The Radicals planned to renew the bill. The Bureau became a political machine that controlled the black vote. Many of the Bureau officials were members of the Union League, a secret organization which taught the black man that their prosperity depended on the Republican Party. President Johnson knew the subversive use of the agency and vetoed the bill. James Speed was disappointed and disturbed that the President did not sign the bill. The veto led to an open rupture between the Republican members of Congress and President Johnson.

Although the courts and the Radicals let Confederate General Robert E. Lee, commander of the Army of Northern Virginia, free and did not try him for treason, Confederate President Jefferson Davis would not be so lucky. On May 10, 1865, the Federal army captured Davis. In July 1865, the cabinet agreed to try Davis for treason rather than murder. Again the question arose as to whether try Davis in a military court or a civilian court. Speed gave his opinion that trials for high treason could not be tried before a military tribunal, only the civil courts had the jurisdiction. Johnson insisted that Speed lead the prosecution. In late July 1865, James Speed, Lovell Rousseau,

William Evarts and John H. Clifford prepared the case. The trial would take place in Virginia. Speed argued that in the Constitution trials must be held in the state and district where the crime had been committed. Speed felt certain that Chief Justice Salmon Chase would sympathize with the government, but Chase refused to become involved in the controversy. Chase referred to district judge, John Underwood, to hold court at Davis's trial, but Speed did not think Underwood was a suitable judge.[303]

While at Fort Monroe, Jefferson Davis wrote to his wife and his lawyer, Charles O'Connor. Speed read all the letters written between Davis and those addressed to O'Connor. He also dealt with the letters between Davis and his wife. The Radicals in the Senate and House passed resolutions asking why Davis was still held in prison and why he had not been brought to trial. The trial was set for April 1866, and Speed called the associate counsel to Washington and made plans to proceed with the case. Davis's counsel attempted to secure bail. On June 7, 1866, O'Connor and ex-governor Thomas Pratt of Maryland waited for Chase to determine whether he would release Davis on bail. Chase referred the question to Underwood, but he refused the counsel's petition. Speed stated that Davis should no longer be denied direct access to counsel and advised the President that Davis's lawyers should be permitted private interviews with Davis. He also suggested that Davis be allowed the freedom to walk the grounds of Fort Monroe. Johnson ordered both recommendations. At this point, Speed's involvement with Davis's trial came to an end.

Speed heard one more case before the Supreme Court involving the case of Lamdin P. Milligan. In the fall of 1864, Federal authorities arrested Lamdin Milligan on a charge of conspiracy. Milligan belonged to the Order of American Knights. The secret society formed in 1863 and had close ties with the Peace Democrats and Copperheads in Indiana. By the summer of 1864, agents fired by Indiana Republicans infiltrated the Knights and discovered a planned conspiracy to seize the Indiana government and turn Indiana to the Confederacy. Indiana Governor Oliver P. Morton used the information gathered by the agents to attack the Democrats in the 1864 elections. Morton ordered troops to seize control of the Knights' press and their

303 Helen Springer, "The Political Career of James Speed," (M.A. Thesis, University of Chicago, Illinois, 1936), 103; Jennifer Cole, "Semper Eadem: An Interpretation of the Life and Career of James Speed," (M.A. Thesis, University of Louisville, 2003), 60.

correspondence. Coverage of the trial against Milligan proved to be a blow against the Democrats and led to a Republican victory in the fall elections in Indiana. A military tribunal convicted Milligan and several of his associates in overthrowing the government and sentenced him to death. The decision and sentence outraged many Indiana citizens, including many Republicans.

Milligan appealed his sentence. At issue was the question of authority of military commissions over civilians. The Supreme Court would decide the validity of military trials of civilians. Speed argued the case for the federal government before the Supreme Court between March 5-13, 1866. Speed and the government argued that the decision of a military commission did have jurisdiction over Milligan since martial law had been declared, that the decision of a military commission could be reviewed only by military authority, and that, if the Court should rule that the commission had no jurisdiction, that the military authorities nevertheless could detain Milligan as a prisoner of war until the war was officially ended, when he might be tried in a civilian court. The Supreme Court disagreed with Speed. They claimed that martial law could not exist if the civil courts were open and functioning. The military tribunal did not have jurisdiction over Milligan or his associates and they were free. Milligan sued the members of the military court for damages from illegal imprisonment. He won the case, but was compensated five dollars, but the more important result of the ruling was the Speed's July 1865 opinion was declared to be wrong.[304] The landmark case Ex Parte Milligan (1866) advanced American civil liberties and the Supreme Court's wariness to give the President and the military arbitrary power.

By late March 1866 Congress adopted the Civil Rights Bill, which gave blacks the right to appear in court, own property, sue and be sued. On March 26, Johnson vetoed the bill. Tension arose between James Speed and President Andrew Johnson over their different views on reconstruction. On March 27, Joshua Speed wrote to his brother James that his position was a delicate one and his opinions or convictions to hold peace would not change. Although the President held different convictions and different opinions, Joshua did not feel that should cause a rift between James and the President.[305]

304 Cole, "Semper Eadem: An Interpretation of the Life and Career of James Speed," 63; Gary Lee Williams, "James and Joshua Speed: Lincoln's Kentucky Friends," 171.

305 James Speed, *James Speed: A Personality*, 89.

Several days later, on April 1, 1866, Joshua wrote to his brother James that he felt James should return to Kentucky. He stated that James Speed had been appointed by Lincoln as a representative man of the party for freedom in the slave states. The country and party were satisfied with his appointment. If James quit, those whose political fortunes and political destiny were linked would mourn his departure and his enemies would rejoice. Joshua advised James to remain in office and never sacrifice his honor. Joshua Speed felt that the progress of freedom could not stop him in the public mind. Andrew Johnson and his whole cabinet may try and stop, but the "wheels of progress will as surely run over them as that they place themselves in the way."[306] On April 9, 1866, Congress overrode Johnson's veto. Johnson told Welles that James Speed "added no strength to the administration, was manifestly in harmony with the Radicals, advising with and encouraging them. Delicacy should cause him feeling as he did, to retire, but he had made no advance in that direction, nor would be, probably, uninvited."[307] To make matters uncomfortable for James Speed, Johnson took his appointing power away from him. Up to that point, James Speed made all the appointments and Johnson accepted them, but Johnson feared that James Speed appointed only men who met his political persuasions.

Early in the month of May, James Speed returned to Kentucky. When he returned to Washington in late May, he faced a showdown between Johnson and the Radicals over the Fenian Brotherhood. The Fenian Brotherhood was an Irish-American group organized in 1858, with the goal of establishing a free and independent government on Irish land. The Fenian Brotherhood resented and irritated over England's support of the Southern Confederacy during the Civil War.

In October of 1865, the Fenian movement held a convention in Philadelphia and the independence of Ireland was declared and a government set up in New York City. The English government became concerned and repealed the writ of habeas corpus in Ireland on January 17, 1866, and arrested the conspirators. The Irish in America planned to attack the British by an invasion of Canada. Meeting points in Malone and Potsdam in New York and St. Albans in Vermont, and Buffalo were set up and ammunitions were gathered and

306 James Speed, *James Speed: A Personality*, 89.

307 Gideon Welles, *Diary of Gideon Welles, Vol. II*, (Boston and New York: Houghton Mifflin Company, 1911).

stored at border points from Buffalo to New York. Stanton wanted Johnston to make a proclamation to put down the Fenian organization. The Republicans hoped to use the political situation against Johnson. Welles feared that if the President acted alone against the Fenians, the Radicals would gain valuable Irish votes in the fall elections. President Johnson passed the problem on to James Speed. On May 1866, at Buffalo, several hundred men gathered, under Major General John O'Neil. On May 31, several hundred men crossed the Niagara to Fort Erie Village. Arms were distributed to the men and pickets sent out. On June 1, 1866, O'Neil received information that Colonel Peacock of the British army was 15 miles north. On June 2, at the Battle of Limestone Hill, O'Neil fought the British Volunteer Regiment of Toronto. The Fenians left the field of battle.

As soon as the Fenians made their way back to the United States, the United States steamer Michigan met them. Once in custody, the administration had no idea what to do with the Fenians. Speed thought that the Fenians were prisoners of the state and released them on bail, but the British ambassador to the United States, Sir Frederick Bruce, wanted Secretary of State William Seward to arrest more of the Fenian leaders. On June 5, 1866, James Speed told his district attorneys and marshals that by the order of the President they were to arrest all of the leading or prominent members of the Fenians, who were guilty of violating the neutrality of the United States.

The next day, Johnson declared his proclamation that he authorized and empowered General George Meade to employ the land and naval forces of the United States to arrest and prevent the Fenians from setting foot on American soil. In his preliminary order, Speed forced Johnson to declare his proclamation against the Fenians. Speed did not want to cooperate with Johnson and the Fenian affair, especially after Johnson did not support black suffrage and vetoed the Freedman's Bureau Bill, the Civil Rights Bill and the Fourteenth Amendment.[308]

During the month of July 1866, James Speed did not plan to attend the Philadelphia Convention and refused to give his approval to the convention. Johnson supporters formed the National Union Convention and demanded that all cabinet members attend the convention to show a sign of loyalty to the President and his reconstruction

308 Williams, 193-195, Springer, 125-132.

plans. The National Union party opposed black equality. Joshua Speed wrote to his brother that there would be two great parties in the country: the Union Party composed of men devoted to the integrity of the government, willing to save the party, and the other was sectional, believing in the Scripture, changing their tactics to suit the changed circumstances and will struggle for power. The Union Party men were devoted to the Declaration of Independence. The other party, acting on prejudice would seek to have their prejudices reflected in all the actions of the government.

On July 10, 1866, Joshua Speed wrote to his brother as what action he would take in the event that Johnson became a candidate for re-election upon a platform he did not approve, because no human being could advise him as to what he should do. He advised his brother to wait out the issue and meet the problems as they arose.

Several days later on July 13, James Speed wrote to his brother that he had a full and frank talk with the President and decided to resign. He resigned because the President did not agree with the Fourteenth Amendment and he did agree with the amendment. The President favored the new party organization, Speed did not. He ranked the duties and rights of a man and a citizen above those of a politician and office holder.[309] On July 16, Speed wrote a short note of resignation to the President:

> Sir: I herewith resign to you the office of Attorney General of the United States. Be good enough, Sir, to accept my thanks for the kindness, consideration, and confidence you have always shown me.

Johnson did not respond to James Speed's resignation. On the day of Speed's resignation, he did not waste any time in offering his house up for sale and all the furniture. He intended to return to Kentucky as soon as possible.

James Speed's stance on black equality and suffrage differed with President Andrew Johnson's. James Speed became a radical Republican and wanted to continue Lincoln's legacy of a free black man. His radical stance on black suffrage led him to quit his job as Attorney General. When James Speed returned home, he continued

309 James Speed, *James Speed: A Personality*, 94-95.

his radical stance on black suffrage and decided to form the Republican Party in Kentucky, in a state that did not want black suffrage and Lincoln's former party. James Speed faced a challenge he could not win.

Chapter Fourteen

James Returns Home

After resigning from President Andrew Johnson's cabinet as Attorney General, James Speed could not stay away from politics for very long. He returned to his Unconditional Union party in Kentucky two weeks before the summer elections. Unfortunately, the Unconditional Union Party did not have a large following. The position for clerk of the Kentucky Court of Appeals was up for grabs, and the Democratic Party nominated a former Confederate sympathizer, and the Unconditional Unionists and Conservatives nominated a Union general. During the election, many Conservatives in the election switched to the Democrats. James Speed watched as the great majority of Kentuckians supported Johnson's National Union movement and many "disloyal" Kentuckians used the movement to establish their own supremacy in state politics. The Democrats won the clerkship for the Court of Appeals and James Speed wrote to General William T. Sherman that Louisville changed little since Sherman took command in 1861. James Speed wrote to Sherman that citizens of Kentucky shouted the names of Lee and Davis, with rounds of applause, while Grant's name elicited hisses. He felt that Kentucky had switched to Confederate hands and feared the Democrats, under the National Union Movements, would gain victories in other states.[310]

To counteract the National Unionist movement, the Radical Republicans called for Northern Republicans and Southern Loyalists to join together at a convention in Philadelphia. On September 3-6, 1866, the delegates from all the states met first in a meeting of congratulation and then formed into two conventions: the northern delegates into one convention and the southern delegates into the other. The southern delegates chose James Speed as their permanent chairman.

310 Gary Lee Williams, "James and Joshua Speed: Lincoln's Kentucky Friends," (Ph.D., Dissertation, Duke University, 1971), 200-201.

When the committee announced James Speed as chairman, all the delegates rose to their feet and applauded for several minutes. Speed addressed the committee and stated that the purpose of the convention was to establish peace, equal justice and equal rights and equal security to every human being in the United States. "With southern men who have seen this great sin of slavery—which some said was the corner-stone of Republican institutions—and say, with Southern men, who have seen slavery, do know not historically, but we know experimentally that it must perish from the face of the earth." He also addressed the National Union convention led by Johnson and stated that the convention did "much that was good; but it was not wholly unmixed good. That convention, as I read history, came here and simply recorded in abject submission, the commands of one man; the loyal Congress of the United States refused to do it. Aye, and if you ever have a Congress in these United States of America, that does not resolutely and firmly refuse, as the present Congress has done to be merely a recording secretary of the tyrant of the White House, American liberty is gone forever."[311] His address to the convention spread throughout the nation. James Speed later denied he used the word "tyrant" and wrote to President Johnson on September 13, 1866, saying he had used the word "tenant."

On September 6, 1866, James Speed helped the committee to draft resolutions and addresses. The address stated that Andrew Johnson's policy "has wrought the most deplorable consequences, social, moral and political."[312] James Speed wanted black suffrage. The border-states delegates, including Kentucky, opposed black suffrage and when the Committee on Unreconstructed States intended to submit a report which included black suffrage, the border delegates protested. James Speed told the border states they had no right to object to the committee's report, since the members agreed that action concerning the unreconstructed states could be taken only by representatives from those states.[313] James Speed left the convention stating he had more important business in Kentucky. The delegates adopted the committee report, including black suffrage, 80 votes to eight. The resolution stated that impartial suffrage and equality

311 Helen Springer, "The Political Career of James Speed," (M.A. Thesis, University of Chicago, Illinois, 1936), 135.

312 Springer, 137.

313 Williams, 205.

before the law would be conferred on every citizen in the states.[314]

Upon James Speed's return to Louisville from Philadelphia, President Andrew Johnson visited the city in August and gave a speech to 15,000 people. The day after Johnson's speech, James Speed arrived in the city, and thought that the President's speech strengthened the rebels in Louisville. He felt that the rebels thought Johnson was on their side. Again, James Speed mentioned in a letter to Stanton that the crowd cheered for Davis and Lee. Johnson's "swing around the circle" campaign ended in dismal failure. Louisville was one of the few cities that gave Johnson a sympathetic welcome. The Republicans won every gubernatorial contest, carried every state legislature, and obtained a majority in every congressional delegation.[315]

On his return to Louisville, James Speed watched with delight as the Republicans won major victories in the elections across the country. He wrote to Senator Charles Sumner that the latest victories in the elections was "most magnificent." James Speed decided to organize a Radical Republican party. He wrote to Sumner that forming the Republican Party in Kentucky was "right hard work, but a labor of love and I am well and hopeful." In the fall of 1866, James formed local meetings throughout the state. He knew that black suffrage would offend many Kentucky Radicals, so he downplayed the issue, but personally he continued to support the cause. He eventually believed that black suffrage and the Fourteenth Amendment was the only hope for Kentucky Radicals.[316]

In January 1867, James Speed spoke to a caucus of the Radical Republican members of the Kentucky legislature. Balloting for United States Senator began and the Radials nominated James Speed. Most of the Radicals feared James Speed's stance on black suffrage might hurt their party's chances of forming an alliance with the Conservatives and dropped after he received only 42 votes. The Radical Party decided to nominate Benjamin Bristow. The Radicals lost and the Conservatives united with the Democrats and re-elected Garrett Davis to the Senate.[317]

On February 26, 1867, a Radical State Convention was held in Frankfort, and James Speed wrote the platform adopted by the

---

314 Springer, 137.

315 Williams, 207.

316 Williams, 207-208; Springer, 138.

317 Williams, 210.

Radical Convention. The Radicals swore to fight the policy and projects of the "rebel Democracy in Kentucky in their effort to render treason respectable at the expense of the brave men who wore the blue, and bared their bosoms to the battle in defense of the Government in its darkest days of trial, and pledge ourselves to front and combat the spirit thus manifested by the 'so-called Democracy' in any shape it may assume." The platform resolved to support the Union party of the United States and opposed themselves to the doctrines of "rebel Democracy" and extended an invitation to all loyal men of all parts of Kentucky cordial cooperation, regardless of all party names. The party wanted to secure justice and protection to all citizens.[318]

On reconstruction, the Radical Republican Party believed in the rights of the loyal people of the United States and wanted to settle the tense relations between the former Confederate states and the Union. They wanted a speedy restoration of the ex-Confederate states to their former position in the Union.[319]

Unfortunately for James Speed, the Radicals faced defeat in the August elections. After their defeat, the Radical party held a convention on August 27 and James Speed watched the state elections throughout the country. The Radicals lost in Maine, California and Montana. The Radicals nominated Joshua Speed to a three-man state executive committee and participated in the spring campaign, in which the major issue was the Fourteenth Amendment. The Democrats ended up winning all nine districts. For all of James Speed's efforts, the Republican held only 10 out of 100 seats in Kentucky's House of Representatives and only seven out of 38 in the Senate. Kentucky voters did not want radicalism or Congressional reconstruction.[320]

On February 27, 1868, the Republicans held a state convention in Frankfort and nominated Ulysses S. Grant for President and James Speed for vice president. James Speed's nomination gained little support and the crowd at the convention gave him only weak and scattering cheers. On May 20, 1868, the Kentucky Republican Party chose Joshua Speed as delegate-at-large at the Republican National Convention in Chicago. During the national convention, Mr. Wood

---

318 Springer, 139.

319 Ibid.

320 Jennifer Cole, "Semper Eadem: An Interpretation of the Life and Career of James Speed," (M.A. Thesis, University of Louisville, Kentucky, 2003), 80; Williams, 210.

of Kentucky presented James Speed's name for nomination for vice president. Mr. Wood stated that during the "darkest days of this Republic, during the rebellion, when everything seemed to threaten the overthrow of the government, Mr. Speed, at the earliest possible period, took his place in the Union Republican Party, and under that banner he has ever fought. There is no man in this Union, who stands higher in the state of Kentucky, than Mr. Speed."[321] Unfortunately, the convention removed James Speed's name after the first ballot. He received only 22 votes from Kentucky. Kentucky cast their votes for Schuyler Colfax of Indiana.[322]

On July 28, 1868, the Fourteenth Amendment was ratified by 28 of the 37 states, and became part of the supreme law of the land. The major provision of the Fourteenth Amendment was to grant citizenship to "all persons born or naturalized in the United States,"[323] granting citizenship to former slaves. Another provision stated that no state would deprive "any person of life, liberty, or property, without due process of law; nor deny any person within its jurisdiction the equal protection of the laws."[324] The right to due process of law and equal protection of the law applied to both the Federal and state governments. James Speed could not have been happier at the passage of the law, but unfortunately, the Fourteenth Amendment failed to extend the Bill of Rights to the states and failed to protect the rights of black citizens.

Although James Speed ran several times for office, he made one last bid for Congress in 1870. He knew he faced defeat, but hoped to keep the Republican Party alive in Kentucky. By February of 1870, the Fifteenth Amendment had passed through Congress by the Radical Republicans to make sure that Southern blacks retained the right to vote. The Radical Republicans felt that the blacks obtained civil and political equality. James Speed could not have been happier with the passage of the Fifteenth Amendment. Unfortunately the Fifteenth Amendment did little to improve the civil and political conditions in the South. Organizations like the Ku Klux Clan, poll taxes, and property requirements kept the blacks away from the polls and the white-supremacist Democrats took power in the Southern states.[325]

321 Springer, 141.

322 Cole, 80, Williams, 214; Springer, 141.

323 U.S National Archives and Records Administration, Washington, D.C.

324 Ibid.

325 Stephen Foster, Fifteenth Amendment, "Blacks Abandoned" Atlas Editions, 1996.

In September 1870 the Kentucky Republican Party asked permission to use James Speed's name as a nominee for State Representative for the Fifth district and stated that James Speed's services to the government during the war for "the suppression of the rebellion and your bold and influential advocacy of "equal rights to all American citizens before the law" are well known in this district, in this State and in the nation."[326] On September 26, 1870, James Speed accepted the nomination. Speed assured his fellow Republicans that he remained steadfast in his support of black suffrage. James Speed ran against Democrat Boyd Winchester.

During the campaign, Speed praised the Fifteenth Amendment and toured several districts hoping to secure the support of enfranchised blacks. James Speed wrote that he thought the time had come "when every man in this country not convicted of crime should have the right to vote." He stated that blacks "should be permitted to testify as a matter of right and justice. I claim that doors and windows of the courthouse should be open alike from all quarters. I claim that a man who has not the right to testify, is not provided with means of self protection. . . . Let me inform you there is not a civilized country on this globe that excludes the negro from its courts of justice except the state of Kentucky. . . I am for justice and equality before the law. With social equality the law has nothing to do. That regulates itself. . . . "[327] During the campaign, Winchester brought up the subject that James Speed owned slaves earlier in his life, implying that Speed made his wealth from the sale of slaves. When James Speed received word of the slander, he attacked the *Louisville Courier* newspaper which printed the statement that he dealt in slaves. The paper also accused John Speed, James Speed's father, of being a slave trader. James Speed admitted that he inherited slaves from his father's will and stated that because of Kentucky's laws, he could not free the slaves in the state, which was not true. He stated that he sold one slave, at her request, to the same man who owned her husband. He also purchased a slave girl at auction, after she begged James Speed to buy her. He stated that his wife, Jane Speed, took care of the girl until her death. James Speed never again commented on his slave ownership.[328]

326 Springer, 142.
327 Ibid., 145.
328 Cole, 82-83.

On November 2, 1870, the *Louisville Courier-Journal*, led by editor Henry Watterson, attacked James Speed on his slave ownership and his actions as Attorney General. Watterson asked that blacks not vote for Speed because of his history of slave ownership. He stated that many of James Speed's recommendations as Attorney General were unconstitutional.[329] The *Louisville Daily Commercial* supported James Speed and printed an editorial from a "Negro" who stated that James Speed was responsible for his own actions, not his father's actions. The writer and other former slaves knew that James Speed did not buy or sell slaves. The writer stated that he knew of James Speed's record on emancipation and black suffrage and testimony rights and that the blacks of Kentucky "know Mr. Speed; they know him to be a . . . liberal minded Christian gentleman; they know that in the darkest days under the old regime any poor, ragged, friendless negro could go to him for counsel and advice, and it was given without money and without price; therefore we will vote for him."[330] On November 8, 1870, the Republicans, supported by the black vote, did better in this election, than previous elections, but the Democrats won all nine seats. James Speed lost the election, with receiving only one-third of the vote in his district. Winchester won by 2,500 votes.

After his loss, James Speed decided to give up running for political office. He attended the National Republican Convention in 1872 and 1876, and served on the Committee on Resolutions. Although James Speed held to his convictions for civil and political equality for blacks and the Federal Constitution eventually added the Fourteenth and Fifteenth Amendments, he paid a heavy price for his support of black rights. Because of his support for black rights, he lost every election since 1865. Kentuckians did not want Radical Republicanism.

For Joshua Speed, politics did not become a major influence over his life, as opposed to his brother. He did serve on the Republican state committee and attended the Republican national convention in 1868, but he never ran for political office. Joshua Speed was more interested in business. After the war, he became a very wealthy man. Joshua and his brother-in-law, James Henning, managed many properties in Louisville, while the owners fought either for the Union or the Confederacy, or fled to places of safety in the South. For a

329 Ibid.
330 Cole, 84-85.

modest fee, Joshua Speed preserved and restored the owner's homes and property. Joshua Speed's first major business ventures was the Louisville Hydraulic Cement and Water Power Company, located in southern Indiana. The Louisville Hydraulic Cement and Water Power Company was one of the largest cement mills in the world. One of Joshua Speed's nephews, James B. Speed, became the largest single investor in the company and led the company's continuing development. After the war, Joshua and his wife Fanny moved to a country home called "Cold Spring" on the Beargrass Creek, near Louisville's Cherokee Park neighborhood. Every day, Joshua Speed rode to his city office in Louisville and Fanny cultivated flowers around the home and in her specially built greenhouse. Joshua Speed built extensive conservatories. Joshua and Fanny never had children.[331]

As Joshua Speed's estate accumulated, he became a civil and business leader in Louisville. He pioneered many public improvements, and became the president of the Louisville and Portland Canal Company from 1872 to 1873, and for two years was the president of the "Short Line" Railroad, also known as the Louisville, Cincinnati, and Lexington Railroad. He was the director in the Louisville and Bardstown Turnpike Company and the Talmage Ice Company. He was president of the Louisville Hotel, director of the Louisville Vault Company; the organizer and director of the Louisville Cement Company; and director of the Savings Bank of Louisville.[332]

In 1874, Joshua and Fanny Speed, accompanied by one of his sisters, visited California. He stopped at Salt Lake City and traveled to San Francisco. On October 15, 1874, Joshua attended the final dedication of the Lincoln monument in Springfield, Illinois. The monument cost nearly $200,000. The monument stands upon a lot of seven acres, donated by the Oak Ridge Cemetery. The statue of Lincoln stands ten feet high. In his right hand is the scroll of emancipation, with the pen he used in signing his name to the document. At his feet is the American Coat of Arms. The laurel, the emblem of peace, is in the talons of the eagle; while the eagle has a broken chain in her beak, representing the broken chain of slavery. On either side of him are

---

331 Robert Kincaid, *Joshua Fry Speed: Lincoln's Most Intimate Friend*, (Harrogate, Tennessee: Lincoln Memorial University, 1943), 31; Williams, "James and Joshua Speed: Lincoln's Kentucky Friends," 217.

332 Kincaid, *Joshua Fry Speed: Lincoln's Most Intimate Friend*, 31; *Joshua Fry Speed, Reminiscences of Abraham Lincoln & Notes of a Visit to California*: two lectures with a sketch of his life, (Louisville: Bradley & Gilbert Company, 1914), 11.

bronze groups of the army and navy, the instruments to preserve the Government and put down the rebellion.[333]

At the unveiling, Joshua Speed described Lincoln's statue covered by an American flag. After his speech, Governor Richard Oglesby turned and pointed to the statue and said: "Behold the image of the man." The vale was withdrawn and shout after shout filled the air from the large crowd, but streams of tears ran from the friends and neighbors who had known Lincoln.[334]

In 1872, James Speed held the position of Professor at the University of Louisville Law School, which he held until 1880. He enjoyed teaching. He also maintained his law practice. He was the senior member of the firm J. T. & Speed, with his son James Speed, Jr., and his cousin Thomas Speed.[335] He bought a home in the country called The Poplars. While at The Poplars, James loved old books and liked old wine. Every morning he would walk out between the lilac bushes then turn down a sidewalk which led by old fashioned flower beds, with roses. He gathered the roses and arranged them into small bouquets on a big table on the huge old back porch. During the spring, summer and fall, every Sunday became guest day at James Speed's home. Neighbors dropped in from the country, and many friends and relatives from Louisville drove out to his house and spent the day under the shade of the trees in the big front yard, and ate dinner. Every Saturday, James Speed gave an enormous roast so that no matter who might drop in for dinner, there would be plenty to eat. At his house on Sunday, 20 or 30 friends and relatives dropped by for dinner.[336]

In 1873, James Speed became involved in a controversy concerning the trial of the Lincoln conspirators, especially Mary Surratt. According to former Judge Advocate Joseph Holt, five of the nine military commissioners signed a note asking for clemency for Mary Surratt. President Andrew Johnson claimed he never saw the clemency note and accused Holt of suppressing the note because Holt wanted Surratt to hang with the rest of the conspirators. He stated that James Harlan admitted that no part of the record was ever read in his presence. He also pointed out that the petition could have not

333 Joshua Speed, 23.
334 Joshua Speed, 23.
335 Cole. 87.
336 Speed Family Collection, Louisville Free Public Library.

been considered in a Cabinet meeting, since he was ill and no meeting had taken place until Friday. Holt claimed that he gave the note to Johnson.[337]

When the controversy arose in 1873, former Secretary of State William Seward and former Secretary of War Edwin Stanton were already dead, and Holt relied on James Speed to bail him out and tell what happened at the cabinet meeting. Speed stated that he had "saw the record of the case in the President's office, and attached to it was a paper, signed by some of the members of the Commission, recommending that the sentence against Mrs. Surratt be commuted to imprisonment for life; and, according to my memory, the recommendation was made because of her sex. I do not feel at liberty to speak of what was said at Cabinet meetings."[338] Johnson continued to state he did not see the note and stated that James Speed was wrong about having seen the petition in the Presidential office, since no one else had been present when Holt and Johnson discussed the trial papers and since Holt took the papers with him after the meeting. Johnson stated that Speed may have seen the paper in the War office. Johnson claimed that Holt purposely withheld the clemency note from him. Holt stated that Johnson spoke out because Steward and Stanton were dead and because Speed's letter indicated that Johnson did not fear the release of any cabinet secrets.[339]

After the failure of his Savings Bank of Louisville in 1881, Joshua and his wife Fanny traveled abroad and vacationed at Nassau, Bahamas, in the winter of 1881-1882. Joshua began to fail in his health with diabetes, and his health did not improve in the Bahamas. He returned home to Louisville in the spring of 1882 and fell critically ill. On May 29, 1882, at the age of 67, he passed away in the Louisville Hotel. According to the *Louisville Courier Journal*, a month before his death, he became a member of the Methodist Church. He left three brothers, James, Philip and Smith, and six sisters. The paper stated that Lincoln urged Joshua Speed to accept an office, but he declined; but "through what is called Mr. Lincoln's undying esteem for the Speed family, his opportunities became very great, throughout the war, for alleviating the sufferings and lessening the hardships which

337 Guy Moore, *The Case of Mrs. Surratt: Her Controversial Trial and Execution for Conspiracy in the Lincoln Assassination*, (Norman: University of Oklahoma Press, 1954), 107-108; Cole, 88.

338 Moore, 107; Williams, 223.

339 Williams, 224.

war brought upon the people of his State; and probably no man knew more perfectly or revered more profoundly the character of Abraham Lincoln."[340] The paper described Joshua Speed as a man of "fine judgment, solid intellectual attainments, of exceptional conversational powers, of fine taste; [he] was possessed of many admirable traits of character; was a successful and upright business man, and was one of the most widely esteemed and valuable citizens of Louisville. There was no one more exact in his justice, even to the minutest questions. He was strong willed, but fair, and his sense of honor was unsurpassed. Hundreds of negroes in and about the city will mourn today for 'Mars Josh.' He was their special friend in time of need."[341] Joshua Speed's funeral took place at the Methodist Church on Third Street, and his wife buried Joshua in Cave Hill Cemetery, not too far from his Cherokee home. At the time of his death, Joshua Speed's estate was valued at $600,000 and the estate was divided between his wife Fanny and his brothers and sisters and their descendents. Fanny did not pass away until August 10, 1902. During her life, she was a devoted member of the Trinity Methodist Church. Her major charity was educational work among the mountain people of Kentucky through her charity at the Methodist Kentucky Conference and helped establish Union College, in Barbourville, Kentucky. She contributed more than $375,000 for expenses, building, and endowment of Union College.[342]

After the death of his brother in 1882, James Speed continued in his law practice, although he gave up his professorship at the University of Louisville. In 1883, Joseph Holt again wrote to Speed and asked him whether he saw the clemency note. Speed did not write back to Holt. Holt became outraged at Speed's silence. Speed wrote to Holt that he would not comment on the note again. Johnson was dead and as far as James Speed was concerned the matter should be dropped, in which he wrote to Holt: "After very mature and deliberate consideration, I have come to the conclusion that I cannot say more than I have said." Holt continued to insist that James Speed eavesdropped on his conversation with Johnson and stated that he had seen the clemency petition.[343]

340 "Joshua Speed Dead," *The Louisville Courier-Journal*, May 20, 1882.
341 Ibid.
342 Kincaid, 31.
343 Moore, 110-111.

In 1885, Jane Speed passed away and James Speed's own health began to deteriorate. In May 1887, James addressed the Society of the Loyal Legion in Cincinnati. In his speech, he declared that Holt performed his duty "kindly and considerably. In every particular he was just and fair. This I knew. But Judge Holt needs no vindication from me or anyone else. I only speak because I know reflections have been made, and because my position enabled me to know the facts, and because I know the perfect purity and uprightness of his conduct."[344] James Speed stated in 1873 that with or without Holt's note, Mary Surratt would have faced the same ending. He stated that Johnson would have hanged Surratt no matter whether he had seen the note or not.[345]

On June 25, 1887, James Speed passed away in his home near Crescent Hill, a few miles from Louisville. When the courts of Louisville heard of James Speed's death, citizens everywhere "received the news with the deepest feelings of regret. Those who had opposed him politically in the past when bitter animosities were engendered wiped out all recollections of such occurrences in respect to his memory and the unblemished life he led." A meeting of the members of the Louisville Bar took action in regard to James Speed's death, and met in the Chancery Court room. The largest amount of lawyers ever held in the city met for the resolution to honor James Speed. During the meeting, Judge A.P. Humphreys moved that the Chair appoint ten members of the bar to act as honorary pall bearers at the funeral, and that the other members be requested to attend in a body. The committee appointed Judge J.W. Barr, Judge Emmett Field, Judge I.W. Edwards, Judge W.S. Jackson, Judge S.B. Toney, Judge W.B. Hoke, Judge J.K. Goodloe, Judge Joseph Kincaid, Colonel T.B. Farleigh, Honorable James Harrison, Isaac R. Green, and Colonel T.W. Bullitt as pallbearers. James Speed's funeral took place at the Church of the Messiah, on the corner of Fourth and York Streets. The body was enclosed in a plain casket, with no flowers. James Speed's casket was carried into the church by Thomas A. Speed, James B. Speed, Joshua F. Speed, Gilmer Adams, E.J. Monahan, and James Pirtle. Behind the relatives came the honorary judges who acted as pallbearers. After the coffin had been placed in the chancel, Rev. Mr. J.K. Jones delivered a brief speech on James Speed's character and

344 Williams, 229.
345 Cole, 89.

personality. The pallbearers took James Speed's body to Cave Hill Cemetery, for a private burial with only relatives present.[346]

The *Louisville Courier-Journal* described James Speed as a man void of all pretense, generous and confiding; was firm in maintaining, what he conscientiously believed to be right, and, while desiring the approval of his fellow men, was ready to support his principles against opposition. His integrity, uniform courtesy and punctilious dealing with members of his profession won for him the highest esteem of all with whom he came in contact. He was a speaker of great force and precaution, often rising to eloquence." James Speed left six living sons, out of seven. The oldest son entered the Union army at the age of 17 and served as a staff officer throughout the war. President Rutherford B. Hayes sent a telegram from Ohio stating: "All who have the privilege of knowing James Speed will unite in most sincere and respectful tribute to his memory. The Ohio Commandery of the military order of the Loyal Legion especially wish to do honor to their beloved companion, whose talents and virtue made him worthy to be the trusted adviser and friend of Abraham Lincoln."[347]

In 1915, the *Louisville Courier-Journal* did a review of James Speed's book on his grandfather, James Speed, entitled *James Speed: A Personality*. Watterson paid tribute to Joshua and James Speed:

> The affinity between James Speed and Joshua Fry Speed was close in the extreme-and beautiful to see. No two brothers ever held nearer together. In their likes and dislikes, in their simple, unconventional pleasures, at work or at play, they displayed the same bent" always moderate but fixed and firm; reserved yet not ungenial; the sense of cast, perhaps only half conscious, but very obvious and not at all intrusive.
>
> Joshua Fry Speed's undervaluation of his intellectual gifts, as Lincoln well knew, amounted to an obsession. He was a very able man. But he lived in the ideal, he had made of James Speed, who had prepared himself for the law and an ambitious career, while he had gone, very successfully be it known, into

346 "Let Him Sleep Full of Rest." *The Courier-Journal*, June 27, 1887.

347 "Gen. James Speed. Death of One of Jefferson County's Most Distinguished Citizens." *The Louisville Courier-Journal*, June 26, 1887.

> trade. James Speed, on the other hand, with perfect confidence in his own judgments, was constrained-one might call it pride–to a fault. He was a man of scrupulous fidelity; sometimes, as those who knew him thought, carrying his conception of personal honor to unnecessary extreme."[348]

After the war, John W, Finnell, Adjutant General of Kentucky during the war, stated that in the earlier days of the rebellion Joshua Speed played

> a very important, but before the general public an inconspicuous part in saving Kentucky to the cause of the Union. He was quiet, observant, courageous man. Full of energy and resource, self reliant, ardently attached to the Union, and fixed in the noble purpose to do his whole duty, letting consequences take care of themselves. . . . He was for the Union under all circumstances, without condition–but he recognized the force and power of our geographical and social connection with the South, and of the prejudices as well which grew out of it. His aim was to hold Kentucky until the sober thought of her people should bring them to see clearly and unmistakably the real designs of the secessionists–the real issue which they presented–when he felt doubly sure that they would never abandon the Union and the old flag. To this end he worked intelligently, earnestly, and persistently, and his influence was felt all over the state. . . . His influence with Mr. Lincoln was potent. He knew that Mr. Lincoln loved Kentucky, and had confidence in the truth and loyalty of her people who had declared for the Union. His mission was uniformly successful. . . . His position was peculiar: without at any time an office, civil or military, he was the trusted confidant, adviser, and counselor of both the civil and military authorities of the State and Nation throughout the rebellion. . . . In my

348 "A Statesman of the Old School, *The Louisville-Courier Journal*, Monday April 12, 1915.

judgment, no citizen of the Commonwealth rendered larger or more important and effective service to the Union cause in Kentucky, during all the dark days of the rebellion, than did that noble gentleman and patriotic citizen: Joshua F. Speed.[349]

349 Joshua Fry Speed, *Reminiscences of Abraham Lincoln & Notes of a Visit to California*: two lectures with a sketch of his life, Louisville, Kentucky: Bradley & Gilbert Company, 1896.

Conclusion

The friendship that developed between Joshua Speed and Abraham Lincoln lasted until Lincoln's death in 1865. Joshua Speed became Abraham Lincoln's closest and intimate friend. The friendship spread to his brother James Speed, who later became Lincoln's Attorney General in 1864. Joshua and James Speed became Lincoln's informal informants on the military and civilian activities during the Civil War in Kentucky. With Lincoln's help, Joshua and James Speed helped save Kentucky for Unionists early in 1861. Both Joshua and James were dedicated to the Union, even though each brother followed different paths. James was a Unionist, emancipationist, abolitionist, and Radical Republican. James entered politics, becoming a state representative and later Attorney General under Abraham Lincoln and later Andrew Johnson. Joshua Speed lived his life as a businessman. Joshua differed from his brother and Lincoln, and did not agree with emancipation. In April of 1861 after the attack on Fort Sumter, Kentucky debated the issue of whether to join the Union or Confederacy. With Joshua and James Speed's loyalty to the Union, Lincoln depended on Joshua and James Speed to help secure Kentucky for the Union. With Joshua and James Speed's help, Lincoln managed to transport thousands of weapons into Kentucky for distribution among the loyal Union Home Guard.

During the war, Lincoln needed trustworthy friends to help him deal with the delicate situation in Kentucky. Both James and Joshua Speed kept Lincoln informed on not only the political affairs in Kentucky, but also the civilian affairs. After Lincoln's death James and Joshua Speed helped to preserve Lincoln's legacy in their own way. James Speed became a Radical Republican and fought to gain equality under the law for blacks, even though most of Kentucky did not want to follow the Radial Republican stance on reconstruction.

Joshua Speed helped to maintain Lincoln's legacy by contributing to his memorial and speaking and writing about Lincoln.

Joshua Speed changed the most through Lincoln's friendship. In 1854, Joshua Speed felt that slavery was a constitutional right. He owned slaves. When Lincoln asked for Joshua's advice on the Emancipation Proclamation, Joshua did not agree with the proclamation, but continued to support Lincoln. By 1864, Joshua realized the goal of Lincoln's administration and turned away from the Democratic party and supported the Unconstitutional Union Party. Because of his friendship with Lincoln, Joshua Speed no longer believed in the institution of slavery and supported his brother in his efforts to eradicate slavery in Kentucky and support Lincoln.

His brother James Speed also changed his opinion on slavery. James Speed started as a emancipationist. James thought that emancipation was a state issue and not a federal issue. He also did not support Lincoln's emancipation proclamation, but with Lincoln's influence, James changed his mind about slavery and felt that emancipation should be a federal issue. He became a abolitionist and after Lincoln's death; he was determined to preserve Lincoln's legacy by assuring that blacks had equal rights under the law. Against the overwhelming tide, James Speed supported the Fourteenth and Fifteenth Amendments and tried to install the Republican Party in Kentucky.

Although the brothers may have disagreed with some of Lincoln's policies and opinions, one fact can not be disputed: their friendship with Lincoln was unwavering during the war, and both brothers did everything in their power to support Lincoln. What more can be said for a true friend, than loyalty, devotion, and support.

Appendix

One son of Captain James Speed, Thomas Speed, moved to Bardstown, Kentucky, but built a business in Shepherdsville and his brother, John Speed, who, inherited the farm land from his father's estate in 1800, established himself in Jefferson County, Kentucky.[350] John Speed married Abby LeMaster, whose two daughters were never married. Abby LeMaster died in 1807, and he married his second wife, Lucy Gilmer Fry, in 1808. Lucy Fry was one of the daughters of Joshua Fry and Peachy Walker, a descendant of Doctor Thomas Walker, neighbor of Fry and Jefferson, godfather and tutor of Thomas Jefferson. Thomas Walker became the first white man to open Kentucky in 1750 to settlers who traveled through the Cumberland Gap. Joshua Fry became one of Kentucky's great teachers and benefactors. Joshua Fry's grandfather, Colonel Joshua Fry of Virginia, was a friend and fellow surveyor of Peter Jefferson, the father of Thomas Jefferson, author of the Declaration of Independence. Lucy Gilmer Fry came to Kentucky with her parents, who settled in Mercer County, Kentucky. John and Lucy Speed had 11 children.[351] In the late 1790s John Speed operated the salt works at Mann's Lick in southern Jefferson County. Many of the laborers were black slaves he hired from other slave owners.

By 1790 Kentucky's population comprised of 12,430 slaves, or 16.9 percent of the total population. Article IX of Kentucky's state constitution legalized slavery, but designed to make the institution as "mild" and humane as possible, compared to plantations in the deep South. In 1794, the first emancipation law allowed the owner to free his slave if he did so in writing, but he must pay a certain fee for the

350 "Louisville First Families," *Louisville Post*, March 15, 1938, Speed Collection, Louisville Free Public Library.

351 Robert Kincaid, *Joshua Fry Speed: Lincoln's Most Intimate Friend*, (Harrogate, Tennessee: Department of Lincolniana, Lincoln Memorial University, 1943.), 12-13.

certificate of freedom and must give a bond for the support of any slave who was unable to take care of himself. By 1830, slaves comprised 24 percent of the population, with seven-tenths of a percent being free. Kentucky's agriculture did not need a large labor force, since the main crops were not cotton, rice, and sugar, which were the main crops in the lower South. The vast majority of Kentuckians did not even own a slave. In 1850, 761,413 whites lived in Kentucky, but only 38,385 owned slaves. In 1850, 139,920 white families lived in Kentucky, but only 28 percent owned one or more slaves. Only five of the owners possessed more than 100 slaves. Twenty-four percent of the average slaveholder owned 5.4 slaves.[352]

In 1809, the income from his successful operation of the salt works helped John Speed to purchase land on the Beargrass Creek. In 1809, John and Lucy Speed and their family lived in cabins. In 1810 John Speed owned 10 slaves and two of the slaves, were Phillis Thurston and her brother, Morocco; both had been previously owned by the Fry family and were given to John and Lucy Speed. Although John Speed owned slaves, he did not like the institution. Reverend John H. Heywood, a Unitarian minister in Louisville, wrote that John Speed "was a slave-owner of the class of slaveholders to which Washington and Jefferson belonged, who neither believed in the system of slavery nor desired its perpetuity, but who, having become such in the circumstances that surrounded them by inheritance or otherwise, endeavored to be thoroughly faithful to the great responsibility incurred."[353] John Speed was not alone in his thoughts about slavery. Henry Clay, the Great Compromiser and Kentucky Whig, also disliked the institution of slavery in theory, but he was also a slave-owner who tolerated the institution as a practical matter.[354]

John Speed devoted his 550-acre plantation to growing hemp. Hemp was used to make rope and bagging for the cotton trade. By 1813, John Speed's hemp became so successful he bought 43 slaves to help on his plantation. He established a self sustaining plantation growing corn, hay, apples, pork, vegetables, wheat, tobacco, and dairy products. John Speed's plantation became the scene of lavish Southern hospitality, which extended not only to his family but also

352 Lowell Harrison and James Klotter, *A New History of Kentucky*, (Lexington: University of Kentucky Press, 1997), 167.

353 Helen Springer, "The Political Career of James Speed," (Master Thesis, University of Chicago, 1936),

354 Lowell Harrison & James Klotter, *A New History of Kentucky*, 112.

friends. During the War of 1812 John Speed entertained entire companies and even larger bodies of Kentucky volunteer soldiers.

In 1815, John and Lucy Speed decided to build their dream house. The original building was the work of Paul Skidmore, a Kentucky entrepreneur. Skidmore was influenced by the architectural work of Thomas Jefferson. With two octagonal rooms imbedded in the center of the house, Farmington's plan is similar to one produced by Thomas Jefferson for an unidentified residence. Master carpenter Robert Nicholson was contracted to build "Farmington." According to the historians at Farmington, Lucy Speed's uncle by marriage George Divers, lived at another house called Farmington. Divers' house in Charlottesville, Virginia, had a Jefferson-designed octagonal addition. Lucy Speed must have seen the house on a trip back to Virginia in 1806. The rooms were large, with high ceilings, deep casements, and tall windows. The woodwork, floors, and casements were of the finest hardwood. A long driveway lined with locust and walnut trees approached the mansion, which set back a quarter of a mile from the Bardstown Pike. In the rear of the home was an avenue which led to the family burying ground, a stone barn, and springhouse. The Federal style house was completed in 1816.

By 1820, John Speed acquired 55 slaves. From then until his death in 1840, Speed never owned less than 50 slaves, and at one point he owned as many as 64 slaves, which placed him as a atypical slaveholder in Kentucky. In 1835, John Speed wrote to his son that his plantation produced a 21-ton crop and he planned to manufacture the hemp into bags himself.[355]

355 Gary Lee Williams, "James and Joshua Speed, Lincoln's Kentucky Friends," 40.

References

Baker, Jean, *Mary Todd Lincoln: A Biography*, New York & London: W. W. Norton & Company, 1987.

Beale, Howard, ed, *The Diary of Edward Bates: 1859-1866*. Washington: United States Printing Office, 1933.

Butler, Loraine, *John Morgan and His Men*. Philadelphia: Dorrance & Company, 1960.

Collins, Lewis & Collins, Richard, *History of Kentucky, Vol. 1* , 1874.

Connelly, Thomas, *Army of the Heartland-Army of Tennessee 1861-1862*, Baton Rouge & London: Louisiana State University Press, 1967, reprint 1983.

Coulter, Merton E., *The Civil War and Readjustment in Kentucky*, University of North Carolina Press, 1921, reprint Glouster, Mass, 1966.

Crist, Lynda, Dix, Mary & Willaims, Kenneth, *The Papers of Jefferson Davis, Volumes 1-9*, Baton Rouge & London: Louisiana State University Press, 1993-1997.

Davis, William C., *Breckinridge: Statesman, Soldier, Symbol*, Baton Rouge & London: Louisiana State University Press, 1974.

Donald, David, *"We Are Lincoln Men": Abraham Lincoln and His Friends*, New York & London, Simon & Schuster, 2003.

____________, *Lincoln*. New York: Simon & Schuster, 1995.

Faust, Patricia, ed., *Historical Times Illustrated Encyclopedia of the Civil War*, Harper & Row Publishers, 1986.

Harrison, Lowell & Klotter, James, *A New History of Kentucky*, Lexington: University of Kentucky Press, 1997.

Harrison, Lowell, *The Civil War in Kentucky*, Lexington: University Press of Kentucky, 1975.

Johnston, J. Stoddard, *Confederate Military History of Kentucky: Kentucky During the Civil War*, ebooksondisk.com, 2006.

Kincaid, Robert, *Joshua Fry Speed: Lincoln's Most Intimate Friend*, Harrogate, Tennessee: Lincoln Memorial University, 1943.

McDowell, Robert Emmett, *City of Conflict, Louisville in the Civil War, 1861-1865*, Louisville: Louisville Civil War Roundtable, 1962.

Moore, Guy, *The Case of Mary Surratt: Her Controversial Trial and Execution for Conspiracy in the Lincoln Assassination*. Norman: University of Oklahoma Press, 1954.

Sears, Richard, *Camp Nelson, Kentucky: A Civil War History*. Lexington: The University Press of Kentucky, 2002.

Speed, James, *James Speed: A Personality*, Louisville: John P. Morton & Com., Inc., 1914.

Speed, Joshua Fry, *Reminiscences of Abraham Lincoln & Notes of a Visit to California: two lectures with a sketch of his life*, Louisville, Kentucky: Bradley & Gilbert Company, 1896.

Steers, Edward, Jr., *Blood on the Moon: The Assassination of Abraham Lincoln*, Lexington: University Press of Kentucky, 2001.

Swanson, James & Weinberg., Daniel, *Lincoln's Assassins: Their Trial and Execution*, Arena Editions, 2001.

Trefousse, Hans, *Andrew Johnson: A Biography*, New York & London: W. W. Norton & Company, 1989.

Welles, Gideon, *Diary of Gideon Welles: Secretary of the Navy under Lincoln and Johnson with an introduction by John T. Morse, Jr., Volume 1-3* Boston and New York: Houghton Mifflin Company, 1911.

Woodworth, Steven, *Jefferson Davis and his Generals: The Failure of the Confederate High Command in the West*. Lawrence: University of Kansas, 1997.

Wilson, Edward & Davis, Rodney O., ed., *Herndon's Informants, Letters, Interviews, and Statements about Abraham Lincoln*, Urbana & Chicago: University of Illinois Press.

Yater, George, *Two Hundred Years at the Falls of the Ohio*. Louisville: The Heritage Corporation, 1979.

The Military Department of Kentucky, *The American Guide Series, The Military History of Kentucky*, Works Projects Administration, 1939.

Articles

Kincaid, Robert, "Joshua Fry Speed-1814-1882 Abraham Lincoln's Most Intimate Friend," Part I & Part II, *Filson Club History Quarterly*, April 1943, Vol. 17, No. 2, 63-89.

______________, "Joshua Fry Speed: Lincoln's Confidential Agent in Kentucky," *The Register of the Kentucky Historical Society*, Vol. 52, April 1954, 99-110.

Springer, Helen, "James Speed, The Attorney General, 1864-1866." *The Filson Club History Quarterly* 11 (July 1937), 169-188.

Dissertations and Theses

Cole, Jennifer, "Semper Eadem: An Interpretation of the Life and Career of James Speed," M.A. Thesis, University of Louisville, 2003.

Messmer, Charles, City in Conflict: A History of Louisville, Kentucky 1860-1865, M.A. Thesis, University of Kentucky, 1953.

Paine, Christopher, "Kentucky will be the last to give up the Union:" Kentucky Politics 1844-1861, Ph.D. Dissertation, University of Kentucky, 1998.

Springer, Helen, "The Political Career of James Speed," M.A. Thesis, University of Chicago, 1936.

Volz, Harry, III, "Party, State, Nation: Kentucky and the Coming of the Civil War, Ph.D., Dissertation, University of Virginia, 1982.

Williams, Gary Lee, "James and Joshua Speed, Lincoln's Kentucky Friends.: Ph.D. Dissertation, Duke University, 1971.

Primary Sources:

Basler, Roy, Collected Works of Abraham Lincoln, 1953, The Abraham Lincoln Association, www.hti.umich.edu.

The Abraham Lincoln Papers, The Library of Congress. Transcribed and Annotated by the Lincoln Studies Center, Knox College, Galesburg, Illinois.

The Joseph Holt Papers, The Library of Congress, Washington, D.C.

The Robert Anderson Papers, The Library of Congress, Washington, D.C.

The Leonidas Polk Papers, 1856-1868, Microfilm, Archival Manuscript Material Collection, The Library of Congress, Washington, D.C.

The Filson Club, Louisville, Kentucky:
John B. Bruner Papers
Farmington Collection
Norvin Green Papers
John F. Jefferson Diary, 1861, 1863
William Nelson Papers
Alfred Pirtle Journal
Firtle and Rogers Families Papers
James Speed Miscellaneous Papers
John Speed Miscellaneous Papers
Speed Family Miscellaneous Papers
Wesley Williams Miscellaneous
Newspapers
Louisville Post
The Louisville Courier-Journal
The Louisville Commercial
The Louisville Courier
The Louisville Journal
Harper's Weekly

Index

D

E

F

G

H

I

J

K

L

M

About the Author

Bryan S. Bush

Bryan Bush was born in 1966 in Louisville, Kentucky and has been a native of that city ever since. He graduated with honors from Murray State University with a degree in history and psychology, and received his master's degree from the University of Louisville in 2005. Bryan has always had a passion for history, especially the Civil War. He has been a member of many different Civil War historical preservation societies, has consulted for movie companies and other authors, coordinated with other museums on displays of various museum articles and artifacts, has written for magazines, such as *Kentucky Civil War Magazine*, *North/South Trader*, and *Back Home in Kentucky* and worked for many different historical sites, and has always fought hard to maintain and preserve Civil War history in the Western Theater. In 1999, Bryan published his first work: *The Civil War Battles of the Western Theater*, which was given good reviews by *North/South Magazine* and *Kentucky Monthly*, which said Bryan Bush's *The Civil War Battles of the Western Theater* "has with his first book created a needed addition to any serious Civil War library." Since then, Mr. Bush has had published *Terry's Texas Rangers: The 8th Texas Cavalry*, *My Dearest Mollie: The Civil War Letters of Brig. Gen. Daniel F. Griffin, 38th Indiana Volunteer Infantry*, *Lloyd Tilghman: Confederate General in the Western Theater*, *Butcher Burbridge*, and was a contributor to *Kentucky's Civil War*. Bryan Bush has been a Civil War reenactor for fourteen years, portraying an artillerist. For five years Bryan was on the Board of Directors and curator for the Old Bardstown Civil War Museum and Village: The Battles of the Western Theater Museum in Bardstown, Kentucky.

More great books from Acclaim Press

One of the most vilified and hated men in Kentucky during the Civil War period had to be Kentucky-born Union (brevet) Major General Stephen Burbridge, but why do Kentuckian historians continue to cast him negatively? *Butcher Burbridge* traces the general's rise to power and his accomplishments on the battlefield, his appointment as commander of Kentucky, his conflicts with Kentucky Governor Thomas Bramlette, and his removal from command in 1865. Read and decide for yourself whether history has been too harsh on Burbridge's legacy in Kentucky.

Lloyd Tilghman was a West Point graduate, soldier, engineer, and family man. Coming to build a railroad, the talented engineer settled in Paducah, Kentucky in 1852. With the advent of the Civil War, the Mexican war veteran followed his convictions south, becoming a Colonel of the 3rd Kentucky Infantry. Promoted to Brigadier General, Tilghman assumed responsibility for the strategically important rivers in western Kentucky and Tennessee. After being taken prisoner follwing the surrender of Fort Henry, he was later exchanged and became an infantry brigade commander. During the Battle of Champion's Hill, while directing artillery fire, Tilghman was struck by a shell fragment and killed, ending a promising military and civilian career.

***In Through the Eyes of Lincoln*,** historian Ron Elliot and award-winning photographer John Snell take the reader on a cross-country journey of the sites and scenery from Abraham Lincoln's rustic birthplace and early homes in Kentucky and Indiana to his military, professional, and political careers in Illinois to Washington, DC and back to his final resting place in Springfield. Elliott's wit and astute observations on each site's role and significance make the perfect, concise companion to Snell's extraordinary ability to capture on film what we all wish we could see. Scores of historic photos are displayed in contrast to today's views coupled with maps, travel directions and recommendations. The first 1,000 copies sold will be a Special Bicentennial Collectors' Limited Edition Printing, hand-numbered and signed by the authors.

In the novel *Freedom's Way*, two pre-Civil War era slaves, Ellen and William Craft of Georgia, devise a brave and cunning plan of escape from their life of bondage that is full of intrigue and peril at every turn of this amazing journey. Could Ellen, who is half white, dressed as a sickly plantation owner going North for "his" health, accompanied by his slave William, ever thread her way through a highly suspicious and adverse territory? Follow their precarious trek as they stay only a step ahead of the slave catchers up the American East Coast, through the Underground Railroad and toward their elusive but undying vision, Freedom.

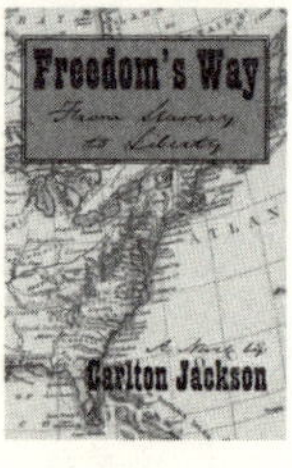

Order today by calling
1-877-4APBOOK
(1-877-427-2665)
or visit www.acclaimpress.com